THE
EGYPTIAN TRAIL
IN
ILLINOIS

A HISTORY FROM CHICAGO TO CAIRO

JAMES R. WRIGHT

THE
History
PRESS

Published by The History Press
Charleston, SC
www.historypress.com

Copyright © 2023 by James R. Wright
All rights reserved

First published 2023

Manufactured in the United States

ISBN 9781467154802

Library of Congress Control Number: 2023934810

Notice: The information in this book is true and complete to the best of our knowledge. It is offered without guarantee on the part of the author or The History Press. The author and The History Press disclaim all liability in connection with the use of this book.

CONTENTS

CONTENTS

PREFACE

This book is an outgrowth of a book I completed in 2009, *The Dixie Highway in Illinois*. While researching that book, I discovered that the Egyptian Trail, an early Illinois auto trail, was "co-aligned" with the Dixie Highway through Homewood, my hometown. With my curiosity piqued, I questioned some longtime residents about this and found 101-year-old lifelong Homewoodian Garrett Tienstra, who was able to confirm firsthand knowledge of the Egyptian Trail. In fact, Garret also advised me that his father, Joseph Tienstra, a painter by trade, was contracted to paint Egyptian Trail marks on telephone poles through Cook County in the fall of 1915. Garrett asked that I try to verify this fact, which I was able to do through old news articles. He was elated that this legacy was documented.

This spurred further research into the Egyptian Trail, with an eye toward writing a book about this long forgotten but historic roadway. Over the course of the last ten years, however, life somehow got in the way with health problems, the coronavirus and other issues, and this endeavor took a back seat.

With renewed vigor and interest in the project, I took up writing in the summer of 2022, and this volume is the result. I hope you will find the book of interest and that it contributes more fully to the transportation history of the state of Illinois.

ACKNOWLEDGEMENTS

M any individuals assisted with the creation of this book, providing photographs and information. These individuals include Kyle Armstrong, Joseph Putnam, Gwen Lagemann (IDOT), Sandra Fritz (Illinois State Library), Cathy Popovitch (Illinois State Archives), Mike Weigler, Dr. Larry McClellan, Georgia Brown (Milwaukee Public Library), Rob Medina, Colleen Layton (Chicago History Museum, Graham Greer (Newberry Library), Steven Wright (Joliet Area History Museum), Homewood Historical Society, John Opyt (Matteson Historical Society), Cheryl Rabe (Onarga Historical Society), Jean Watson (Ford County Historical Society), Savannah Donovan (Urbana Park District), Sara Bennett (Urbana Free Public Library), Perry Morris, T.J. Blakeman (Champaign County History Museum), Anna Dvorachek (Douglas County Museum), Chris Suerdieck (Mattoon History Center), Delaine Donaldson, Jane Ries (Effingham County Museum), Rick Switzer (Farina), Luann Tamborini (Fayette County Museum), Nick Quigley (Jackson County Historical Society), Anna Forby and Lynn Forby Geske (Cobden), Patrick Brumleve and Jean Travelstead (Union County Historical Society, Cobden) and Peter Kaha and Jim Fredlund (Cairo Historical Preservation Project).

Finally, I would like to thank Nancy Dubetz for captioning assistance and Mark Leschuck for his invaluable editorial, scanning and transportation assistance.

INTRODUCTION

Though the Egyptian Trail is almost unknown today, the *Harvey Tribune*, in its October 15, 1915 edition, touted it as being "a distinctive Illinois project in every way for one end is at Cairo, away down in Egypt, at the extreme southern end of the state and the other end is at Chicago, the metropolis of the state in the north." The Egyptian Trail was the concept of two Mattoon men who felt an improved road following as closely as possible the tracks of the Illinois Central Railroad and linking the southern reaches of the state with Chicago was a necessity. These men, Dr. Iverson A. Lumpkin and Ernest B. Tucker, quickly set about organizing an association and promoting the trail to communities in the state.

Interested communities were invited to Mattoon for an organizational meeting of the Egyptian Trail Association held on June 15, 1915, and hundreds from across the state turned out to attend. As a result of the meeting, a decision was made to separate the oversight of the trail into three divisions. The southern division stretched from Cairo to Centralia, the central division extended from Centralia to Paxton and the northern division reached from Paxton to downtown Chicago. Each division had its own president and secretary-treasurer, and each town the trail passed through appointed a vice president who was responsible for helping select the route of the trail in their area, raising funds to "blaze" or mark the trail and seeing to it that the roadbed was maintained in good condition.

The Egyptian Trail Association, the consortium of communities the road passed through, set up rules governing road maintenance and uniform signage. The route was blazed, or marked, by trail signs, generally painted on telephone poles. The Egyptian Trail mark was an orange 12" x 18" sign painted on poles six feet from the ground. In the center of the sign, a black pyramid was painted, flanked by the letter *E* on its left and the letter *T* on its right, both painted in black. The association also called for the placement of signs marking dangerous curves, turns, intersections and rail crossings.

In Chicago, the Egyptian Trail originated at Michigan Avenue and Jackson Boulevard and traveled south on Michigan Avenue to Garfield Boulevard, then west to Halsted Street. The trail continued south on Halsted Street through the city to Harvey, then on to Homewood and Matteson, where it entered Will County and continued south along the Illinois Central Railroad line, passing through Kankakee, Paxton, Champaign, Mattoon, Effingham, Salem, Centralia, Carbondale and points south on the way to Cairo. The total trail route covered over four hundred miles and passed through twenty counties!

Unlike its more celebrated cousins, the Lincoln and the Dixie Highways, the Egyptian Trail was not the subject of grand marketing tours, dedication parades and the like. Trail officials were hardworking Illinoisans who simply rolled up their sleeves and went to work with little fanfare. Their efforts proved successful, as the trail was virtually completely marked by the end of 1915, and the Egyptian Trail Association reported most roads selected to compose the trail were graded and "in shape" by the summer of 1916.

The Egyptian Trail was well traveled during its heyday and lived up to the accolades bestowed on it by the *Harvey Tribune*. The trail route was such a success that most sections were selected to be further improved as part of a $60 million statewide road improvement bond issue overwhelmingly approved by Illinois voters in 1918.

By the mid-1920s, colorfully named auto trails and highways lost favor with state highway officials nationally and, in Illinois, in favor of route numbers. Today, US Route 45 for much of the way from Kankakee to Effingham, Illinois Route 37 from Effingham to Salem, US Route 50 from Salem to Sandoval and US Route 51 from Sandoval to Cairo follow many alignments formerly known as the Egyptian Trail in Illinois.

Although there are only a few areas where original road alignments bear the name of the Egyptian Trail in the state, the impact and foresight of the trail organizers has been longstanding. The Egyptian Trail route served as the basic template for Interstate 57 through Illinois. Fully completed in

December 1971, Interstate 57 runs from just north of Cairo through the heart of Little Egypt in southern Illinois to the south side of Chicago, still that "great metropolis of the north."

Though it is almost forgotten today, a greater appreciation of its history and impact may bring the Egyptian Trail some well-deserved recognition in the future.

Chapter 1

ILLINOIS AT THE DAWN
OF THE MOTOR AGE

Today, we take for granted how well we can travel from place to place over good roads that allow for speeds of over seventy miles per hour, in automobiles that are relatively maintenance-free and, in many cases, have navigation systems to help us on our way. Sure, there are potholes, road construction projects and traffic tie-ups that may be annoyances, but for the most part, our trips, even for long-distance travel, go smoothly.

At the beginning of the twentieth century, this was not the case. Most people still traveled by horse and carriage, and their trips were generally confined to a few miles from their homes. Most roads were dirt roads, and while they were passable in fair weather, they quickly became impassable mud holes after a few hours of rain. More often than not, they were a mess of ruts and potholes. Longer-distance trips were made by train, and people had to adhere to the railroad timetables and routes to make their trips possible.

The Illinois Central Railroad, chartered in 1851, was the first land-grant railroad in the United States. Completed in 1856, it was one of the longest railroads in Illinois at the time. Though it was one of the first in the state, it certainly would not be one of the last. Between 1850 and 1860, railroad mileage in Illinois increased from 100 to 2,790, and this number increased even more dramatically in ensuing decades. Railroad mileage peaked in Illinois in 1925 at just over 12,500. There was no question that with railroads crisscrossing every part of the state, they were the transportation juggernaut in Illinois, and as a consequence, Illinois ignored its roads. The dirt roadways of 1900 were scarcely better than those of 1818—the year

Typical roadway scene after a period of rain. *Illinois Department of Transportation (IDOT).*

of Illinois statehood—and were wholly incapable of handling any surge coming from automobile traffic.[1]

As a stark example of this, Governor Edward Dunne reported in a 1913 address to the Illinois General Assembly that of the estimated ninety-five thousand miles of roads in Illinois, only 10 percent were improved in any "permanent manner." Compared to the rest of the country, Illinois ranked number twenty-four from the standpoint of improved roadways.[2]

To rectify these conditions, organizations such as the League of American Wheelmen, founded in 1880, began to lobby for improved road conditions as early as the 1890s. The Wheelmen were actually an association of bicyclists who began to advocate for good roads long before the advent of the automobile. In the mid-1880s, bicycling became popular after the development of the mass-produced, chain-driven safety bicycle; over one million bicycles were being manufactured in the country each year. The biggest problem for bicyclists was that outside towns and cities, the nation's bad roads made bicycling a laborious, if not dangerous, pastime.[3]

After the turn of the century, other organizations became involved in these lobbying efforts, including the National Good Roads Association, organized in 1900 in Chicago with representatives from thirty-one states; the American Automobile Association, established in 1902; and various automobile tourist clubs, which were originally formed to promote the automobile for recreation but also became lobbying groups for new road construction.[4]

Farmer's organizations as well became outspoken advocates of road construction, not for recreational purposes but to lower the costs of marketing and improve access to their farm products. The federal government, especially the Post Office Department, became another advocate for improved roads. The establishment of Rural Free Delivery, beginning in 1896, was a major

Governor Edward Dunne was a strong proponent of good roads during his term in office. *Library of Congress.*

Railroads were the prime method of transportation at the beginning of the twentieth century. This is an Illinois Central timetable from that period. *Author's collection.*

influence in the federal government promoting the construction of higher-quality stone roads to replace the dirt paths their carriers encountered on rural routes.

Railroads got on board, too. Early on, railroad company officials saw road improvements as being in their own interest, as roadways were viewed as feeders bringing passengers and freight to their depots. The easier this could be done, the better for all.

As a further show of support from railroads, Colonel William H. Moore, president of the National Good Roads Association, convinced a number of the larger railroads in the country to participate in a project called the Good Roads Train. A skillful promoter, Moore conceived this idea of a "traveling good roads show that would cover the country, educating the public on the advantages of improved highways, very much in the manner of circuses and the popular Chautauqua shows" of the time.[5]

Road machinery companies were persuaded to donate their latest equipment, along with trained operators to run it, to put on actual roadbuilding demonstrations in the towns the trains stopped in. The railroads provided the transportation. Advance men visited demonstration locations to line up labor and material donations and generate publicity to ensure good attendance at these shows. Moore also persuaded Martin M. Dodge, the director of the U.S. Office of Public Road Inquiry, to provide a road expert to lecture on roads and supervise demonstrations of roadbuilding at each location during these trips.[6]

Coincidentally, the first Good Roads Train ran on the Illinois Central line from Chicago to New Orleans from April 20 to July 27, 1901, with director Dodge of the U.S. Office of Public

Bicycling groups were also early proponents of good roads. *Author's collection.*

Left: Logo of the American Automobile Association. *American Automobile Association.*

Below: Rural Free Delivery carrier on rounds on a country road. *Library of Congress.*

Road Inquiry along for most of the way. In the annual report of this agency from 1901, Dodge provided this summary of the trip:

> *The "good-roads train" visited the following places, where sample roads, varying in length from a half mile to 1½ miles, were built and where the officers of the National association organized permanent local and State associations: Flossmoor, Ill.; New Orleans, La.; Natchez, Vicksburg, Greenville, Clarksdale, Oxford, Granada, McComb City, and Jackson, Miss.; Jackson, Tenn.; Louisville, Hopkinsville, and Owensboro, Ky.; Cairo and Effingham, Ill.*

Flossmoor, Illinois, railroad depot built in 1901. *Homewood Historical Society.*

About 20 miles of earth, stone, and gravel roads were built and 15 large and enthusiastic conventions were held. The numbers attending these conventions and witnessing the work were very large, in nearly every instance more than a thousand persons and in some cases 2,000 persons being present. Among the attendants were leading citizens and officials, including governors, mayors, Congressmen, members of legislatures, judges of the county court, and road officials. This was undoubtedly the most successful campaign ever waged for good roads, and the expedition has been of great service to the cause, and especially to the people of the Mississippi Valley.[7]

Of note, the Illinois locations visited would later become Egyptian Trail communities. It is also interesting to note that the train started at Flossmoor, Illinois. Located twenty-five miles from downtown Chicago, Flossmoor was unincorporated at the time. It was home to the Homewood Country Club (renamed Flossmoor in 1914), and the Illinois Central owned 160 acres in the area that it had platted into a subdivision for exclusive home sales

Martin M. Dodge, director of U.S. Office of Public Roads Inquiry. *Federal Highway Administration.*

earlier in the year. The railroad likely saw the Good Roads Train stop there as a good way to improve access to and sales of their homesites.

With the railroads, all these groups and others coalesced into what was called the Good Roads Movement, which lobbied local, state and federal legislatures in the effort to improve the conditions of roadways throughout the country. Improved roads generally ended at a city or town limit, and the Good Roads Movement wanted to extend the brick, macadam or concrete roads past those limits to benefit commerce, agriculture and tourism.

Remaining reluctant to act, Illinois's legislature had not addressed the topic of its highway system since a short-lived and underfunded road improvement program in 1871. Growing public sentiment acknowledging the need to "pull Illinois out of the mud" finally shook the state out of its inaction.

In 1903, Illinois became one of the first states to establish a commission to address its roads. On May 15, the Forty-Third General Assembly granted the governor authority to appoint a three-man Good Roads Commission. The commission members were charged with investigating "the various problems of road building in Illinois, such as the best and most economical native materials" and the best method of paying for a statewide highway system.[8]

Shortly after the commission's creation, it was even granted the authority to employ convict labor from the Joliet and Menard state penitentiaries to produce broken stone, drain tiles and road machinery to help supply these necessary roadbuilding materials to districts statewide. In 1913, the law was expanded to allow use of convict labor on road construction projects.[9] Use of convict labor not only would help reduce the costs of construction materials but was also seen as a "humanitarian" way of dealing with the prisoners, giving them an opportunity to work "on the honor system in the fresh air and sunshine, whereby they are restored to society with their manhood quickened, instead of deadened, or destroyed."[10]

The commission's first report was presented to the General Assembly in 1905 and shed light on the dismal state of Illinois's roads. It reported that, estimating the total mileage of Illinois's wagon roads at over one hundred thousand miles, between 1880 and 1900, less than thirty miles of surfaced roads had been constructed! To address these concerns, the report

Joliet prisoners working in prison quarry. *Joliet Area Historical Museum.*

recommended the creation of a permanent state highway commission and a state highway engineer to encourage road and highway improvement.[11]

The commission's reports were highly detailed and illustrated and not only covered their meetings but also gave reports from township highway commissioners and local road improvement associations, provided traffic census information and discussed best construction and improvement practices for various road types and bridges.

In the commission's second annual report from 1907, it recommended, curiously, that "through" roads were not required despite Good Road advocacy to the contrary. The report stated:

THROUGH ROADS NOT REQUIRED

There is a plan about which much is heard, but which does not seem to meet the economic needs of this State, and that is the construction of through roads. Whatever may be the future development of road traffic in this State, such roads are not today required. If any evidence were necessary, the traffic census taken by the State Highway Commission, which shows that the majority of the travel of today is on the first few miles from a given center, demonstrates that through travel practically does not exist. What is first needed is the development of roads around the various centers, and when this has been accomplished it will be full time to take up the question of through roads, if then required.[12]

The question of scope and distance for road improvement was not the only issue in dispute. As one might expect, another major issue was funding. In fact, the two were intertwined. Townships were established in Illinois in 1850, and each of these 1,432 units of government was largely responsible for the construction and improvement of roads in its jurisdiction, which typically consisted of an area of thirty-six square miles. Elected township highway commissioners had a parochial view of their duties, and there was little interest in coordination of activities between adjacent townships. As long as this form of governance and funding was the norm, Illinois roads would continue to rank as poor, with little connectivity.[13] Local roads were still the focus of the government, and Good Road boosters realized more advocacy work was needed to change this.

Slowly, change occurred. In 1907, the Illinois General Assembly approved Illinois's first motor vehicle law. The act, one of the earliest of its kind, defined motor vehicles for the first time and required all drivers to register their vehicles through the secretary of state. For a cost of two dollars per vehicle, drivers were issued "dash disks" that displayed the vehicle's registration year and number. The act also set the state's first speed limit into law.[14]

Registration after the Motor Vehicle Act of 1907 reached twenty-two thousand vehicles within a year. Pleased by the influx of registration funds, legislators amended the law in 1909 to include motorcycles and made vehicle registration annual. In 1910, the Road and Bridge Fund was created using receipts from vehicle registration fees, and vehicle registration fees were increased from two dollars to between four and ten dollars, depending on the vehicle's horsepower.

Actual license plates were issued beginning in 1911. That year, 38,629 licenses were issued with fees totaling $105,344. By 1924, that number had grown to 1,132,641 licenses issued since 1911 with over $11,546,206 generated, which helped to fund road and highway improvements over those years.[15]

Original Illinois license dash disc. *Illinois Secretary of State.*

To better coordinate their activities, Illinois good roads groups banded together to form the Illinois Highway Improvement Association in 1912. The stated goal of the association was "the improvement of the public wagon roads of Illinois, to the end that an adequate and efficient system of road construction, administration and maintenance will be adopted."[16]

Illinois Highway Improvement Association attendees from 1912 convention. *Illinois Highway Improvement Association.*

The group held a convention in Peoria in September 1912 and passed a resolution demanding a bill in the next session of the general assembly to again address the road issue in Illinois. Their pressure on the state legislature led directly to the passage of the Tice Road Law of 1913—named after the legislation's sponsor, Greenview representative Homer J. Tice, a farmer and good roads enthusiast. It established the State Highway Department and finally solidified the state's role in financing public highways. To finance road improvements, the new law authorized state aid to county superintendents for up to half the cost of construction on approved projects.[17] This was seen as a major breakthrough in finally improving Illinois roads.

Despite this optimism, Governor Dunne was forced to report on some of the problems experienced after three years of operation of the law in a report to the Illinois legislature on January 3, 1917. Dunne reported that based on statistics from the state highway commission, "in 1914, 48.32 miles of brick and concrete roads were completed at a total cost of $1,259,911.18; in 1915, 72.38 miles of brick, concrete, macadam, gravel and earth roads were completed at a total cost of $958,839. During 1916, 284.87 miles were constructed, to cost, as awarded, $1,660,114.87." At this rate, the pace of road improvement was going to take forever, and something else needed to be done.[18]

Good roads advocates continued to press ahead, and many business and community groups took matters in their own hands. During the second decade of the twentieth century (1910–19), a number of "marked" trails and highways were routed through Illinois. These were developed by groups like the Lincoln Highway Association (1913) and the Dixie Highway Association (1915), two early "interstate" routes, and also by groups that promoted "intrastate" routes in Illinois like the Starved Rock Trail (1914), the Pontiac Trail (1915), the Caterpillar Trail (1917) and even one named the Swastika Trail (1915).

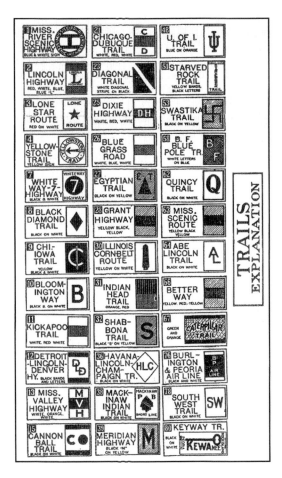

Trail mark guide from State of Illinois road map. *Illinois Secretary of State.*

Where the state was lacking in road improvement progress, these highway and trail organizations picked up the slack and worked to improve the roads along the routes selected between the communities they served. Most times, this work was done as a grassroots effort with little or no government assistance.

Contrary to the Illinois Highway Commission's opinion in 1907 that through routes were not required, in 1916, the Illinois State Highway Department noted in an article in *Illinois Highways* magazine that:

> *A few years ago, such a thing as a route definitely named and marked for the guidance of the traveling public was unknown. Roads were known locally, and were considered only from a local standpoint. The possibility of a road having a relation to other states or the country at large was not realized.*

Consequently, the conditions of roads in various communities have depended upon the enterprise and progressiveness of those communities alone. Since the era of the automobile, with the attending promotion of marked through routes, a great impetus has been given to the improved roads movement. The organized interests of the through route associations have assisted isolated communities and have induced them to improve their roads....

From the standpoint of the automobile tourist the through routes marked at frequent intervals by some conspicuous sign are very desirable. Traveling is much more pleasant when there is no danger of losing the way. Likewise, hotel and garage accommodations are much better for the tourist if the bulk of the traffic proceeds along one route.

To make sure there was no misunderstanding, the article included this statement: "The State Highway Department is heartily in sympathy with the movement to establish marked through routes because in this manner the cause of better roads is served."[19] Support the marked highways the Illinois Highway Department did, and at one time, there were fifty-one named highways recognized by the department in the state of Illinois.[20]

THE LINCOLN AND DIXIE HIGHWAYS

Two of the most prominent marked highways in Illinois were the Lincoln Highway and the Dixie Highway. In fact, these two highways crossed just south of Chicago in Chicago Heights, which is known as the Crossroads of the Nation to show this historical significance. Though Chicago Heights

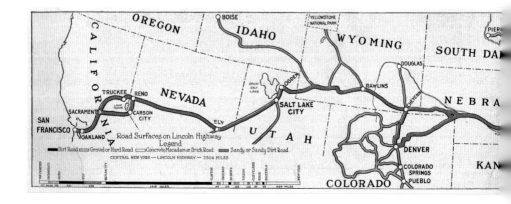

was not an official Egyptian Trail community as it was not on the Illinois Central Railroad line, Western Avenue, now the city's western border, was a part of the Egyptian Trail and intersected the Lincoln Highway about one and a half miles west of the center of Chicago Heights and the Dixie Highway intersection.

Lincoln Highway

Carl Fisher, dubbed the Father of the Lincoln Highway, was a man who turned dreams into reality. Fisher, an Indiana native and entrepreneur, owned the Prest-O-Lite Company, which manufactured compressed acetylene gas headlight systems that made night driving possible. Fisher was an organizer of the Indianapolis Motor Speedway and also had extensive real estate holdings in Florida in what is now the Miami Beach area. An auto enthusiast, he believed that "the automobile won't get anywhere until it has good roads to run on."

In 1912, he began actively promoting his dream of a transcontinental rock highway from New York to San Francisco that he hoped would be completed by May 1, 1915, in time for the Panama-Pacific International Exposition in San Francisco. He estimated the project would cost about $10 million. On September 10 that year, he held a dinner meeting with many of his automobile industry colleagues in the Deutsches Haus in Indianapolis, his hometown, pitching his idea and trying to raise funds.

Map showing the Lincoln Highway across the United States. *Lincoln Highway Museum.*

Within a month, Fisher's auto industry friends, including Frank Seiberling, president of Goodyear, and Henry Joy, president of the Packard Motor Car Company, had pledged $1 million to the project. Henry Ford, the biggest automaker of the day, was a notable exception. He refused to contribute, believing the government, not private individuals or companies, should build the nation's roads.

By July 1913, Fisher and his associates had chosen a name for the road, the Lincoln Highway, after one of Fisher's heroes, Abraham Lincoln. The Lincoln Highway Association dedicated the route on October 31, 1913. Bonfires and fireworks marked ceremonies in hundreds of cities in the thirteen states along the road. In ensuing years, the highway was improved, but by the time the Lincoln Highway Association disbanded at the end of 1927, it was never completely the coast-to-coast "rock highway" Fisher envisioned, with some western sections still remaining to be paved.

The Lincoln Highway runs coast to coast from Times Square in New York City west to Lincoln Park in San Francisco, originally through thirteen states: New York, New Jersey, Pennsylvania, Ohio, Indiana, Illinois, Iowa, Nebraska, Colorado, Wyoming, Utah, Nevada and California. The first officially recorded length of the entire Lincoln Highway in 1913 was 3,389 miles. Over the years, the road was improved and numerous realignments were made, and by 1924, the highway had been shortened to 3,142 miles. Counting the original route and all the subsequent realignments, there has been a grand total of 5,872 miles.

The Egyptian Trail and the Lincoln Highway shared a co-alignment for about a mile and a half, between Chicago Heights and Matteson from Western Avenue to Main Street.[21]

Dixie Highway

Buoyed by the success of the Lincoln Highway, Fisher, who had business interests in real estate in Florida, envisioned a highway that would run from Chicago to Miami, bringing northerners south in the winter and southerners north in the summer. Altruistically, another important goal, and one often forgotten about today, was the intent of highway organizers to have the road serve as a unifying force for the north and south in a country that, only fifty years before, had seen the end of the Civil War, the most divisive event in the nation's history. Thus, the concept of the north–south Dixie Highway was born.

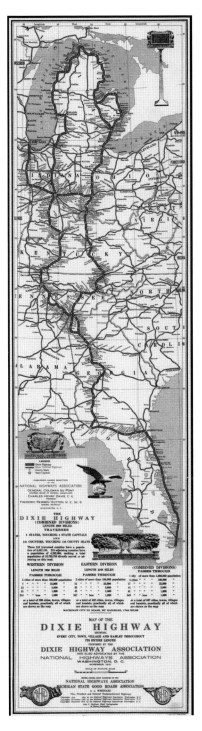

The Dixie Highway was actually a system of interconnecting roads that wound its way through the eastern and middle part of the country. Rather than one distinct route, a decision was made to designate two routes of the highway. The Western Division began in Chicago and traveled through Indianapolis, Nashville and Atlanta on its way south. The Eastern Division started in Sault Ste. Marie, Michigan, and took travelers through Detroit, Toledo, Cincinnati and Lexington on its way to the southern terminus of both divisions in Miami Beach. Later, a branch of the highway extended into North and South Carolina, and the northern terminus of the Western Division became Sault Ste. Marie also.

In Illinois, the Dixie Highway started in downtown Chicago at the foot of the Art Institute on Michigan Avenue and ran south to Garfield Boulevard/Fifty-Fifth Street, then turned west to Western Avenue. The route continued south on Western Avenue into Blue Island, joined the present route of the Dixie Highway through Chicago Heights, and followed present-day Route 1 through Crete, Beecher, Grant Park, Momence and points south to Danville, where the highway heads east on Main Street to the Indiana border, a distance of about 136 miles. By August 1921, the full length of the Dixie Highway in Illinois, from Chicago to Danville, was either concrete or brick paved. This was the longest continuous paved road in the state at the time.

Map showing the route of the Dixie Highway. *Library of Congress.*

The Dixie Highway was marked with distinctive red-and-white "DH" signs. They were painted on poles and fence posts to guide motorists along their way. In the late 1920s, numbers began to replace names in the growing highway system. The Dixie Highway Association disbanded in 1927, but only after 5,786 miles of roadway had been improved in ten states on the two divisions and interconnecting routes of the highway.

The Egyptian Trail and the Dixie Highway shared co-alignments in Chicago from Jackson Drive to Garfield Boulevard/55th Street on Michigan Avenue and in Homewood from 175th Street south through Flossmoor to Illinois Street (Flossmoor Road).

Chapter 2

THE EGYPTIAN TRAIL
AND THE MEN BEHIND IT

T he Egyptian Trail Association was another one of the named highway groups organized to address the good roads issue in Illinois. The Egyptian Trail was a proposed route that would travel the length of Illinois from Chicago to Cairo, a distance of over four hundred miles, following as closely as possible the tracks of the Illinois Central Railroad. The Egyptian Trail was the brainchild of two Mattoon men, Dr. Iverson A. Lumpkin and Ernest B. Tucker, who were keen boosters of their east central Illinois city and ardent automobile enthusiasts. In fact, both men were involved in the establishment of the Big Four Trail in May 1915, which was routed from Terre Haute, Indiana, to Alton, Illinois, and the Kickapoo Trail from Peoria to Evansville, Indiana, in June 1915, both of which passed right through Mattoon.

Dr. Iverson A. Lumpkin, the elder of the two, was born on June 30, 1843, in Miller County, Missouri, where he received his early education. He came to Illinois in 1863 to work on the Terre Haute and Alton Railroad before a chance meeting landed him a position as a photographer's apprentice in Shelbyville. When the photographer saw how fast he could pick up a new trade, he decided to train Lumpkin to replace him in his other occupation as a dentist. Lumpkin married Margaret Cutler on December 24, 1864, in Shelbyville. The couple had one child, a son, William C., who was born on March 24, 1872. In 1885, the family relocated to Mattoon, where Dr. Lumpkin practiced his profession for many years. William would follow in his father's footsteps and became a dentist, too.[22]

Left: Portrait of Dr. Iverson A. Lumpkin. *Right*: Dr. William C. Lumpkin. *Ben Lumpkin.*

Dr. Lumpkin and his son were astute businessmen, with interests in real estate and local banking. They also did not shy away from investing in nascent technologies. In 1894, they were convinced that Alexander Graham Bell's telephone, invented only eighteen years before, would play an important role in the future of Mattoon. Earlier efforts to provide telephone service to Mattoon had failed. A subsidiary of the Bell System's Central Union Telephone Company started operations with one switchboard and twenty subscribers in 1881, but within three years, operations were suspended. Over the next few years, other attempts met similar fates. But by 1894, the original Bell patents had expired, making it possible for independent telephone companies to be formed.

On August 10, 1894, the Mattoon Telephone Company was incorporated, with Dr. I.A. Lumpkin serving as the first president and his son serving as treasurer. On September 4, 1894, the City of Mattoon passed an ordinance granting the new company the right to operate, and the business prospered to the extent that Dr. William Lumpkin later ceased practicing dentistry to devote his time fully to managing the telephone company operations.

The pair organized the Coles County Telephone Company in 1897, which, along with the Mattoon Telephone Company, merged to form the

Dr. Lumpkin supervising telephone switchboard operators. *Consolidated Communications.*

Southeastern Telephone Company and eventually became Consolidated Communications, a company that still exists today.[23]

In 1911, the Lumpkins collaborated again on a new business venture, this time in automobiles. That year, Dr. William Lumpkin established the Mattoon Motor Car Company. Selling only Rambler autos, manufactured by the Thomas B. Jeffery Company of Kenosha, Wisconsin, at first, the dealership soon branched out and also sold Hudsons and the Hupmobile, an automobile brand of the Hupp Motor Car Company of Detroit.[24] Despite a fire that damaged the dealership building and destroyed the cars in it in 1913, this business venture was another success and was operated by the Lumpkins until they sold it in 1922.[25]

Tragically, Dr. William C. Lumpkin died in a one-car auto accident on January 11, 1924. Newspaper reports indicated the crash occurred less than a mile from his home in Mattoon when his "big Packard automobile" skidded on a snow-covered roadway, catapulted off a subway embankment and overturned, crushing him.[26] His father, Dr. Iverson Lumpkin, died due to "the complications of old age" at the age of eighty-seven on July 22, 1930. His obituary noted he "maintained his interest in good roads until the last."[27]

Ernest Buford Tucker, Dr. Iverson A. Lumpkin's cohort in the Egyptian Trail Association, was a native of Paris, Illinois, born on August 4, 1877. His father, Rudolph, died when Ernest was a "child in arms," and shortly thereafter, he and his mother, Clara, moved to Mattoon, where Ernest would live the rest of his life. He was trained as a printer and worked for many years in this occupation at the various newspapers in Mattoon. In 1899, while he was working as a foreman in the printing plant of the *Mattoon Weekly Gazette*, an opportunity presented itself whereby he acquired half interest in this enterprise. By 1905, he and his partners had acquired the *Mattoon Daily Journal Gazette*, and in 1919, they acquired the *Mattoon Commercial Star*. These newspapers merged to form the *Mattoon Daily Journal*. Tucker would initially serve as secretary-treasurer of the Mattoon Journal Company and, later, its president.[28]

Tucker married Mary McBride of Mattoon in 1898, and the couple had no children. Active in community affairs, he was president for a time of the Mattoon Association of Commerce and a member of the Rotary Club, Elks Club, Knights of Pythias and Dramatic Order of the Knights of Khorassan.[29]

Perhaps nothing shows Tucker's enthusiasm for the automobile and good roads more than an article he wrote for the *Rambler Magazine*, a publication of the Thomas B. Jeffery Company for their customers, in September 1905. That spring, Tucker had purchased a single-cylinder, eight-horsepower Model H Rambler. This certainly indicates he was an early adopter of the "newfangled" automobile. The article chronicled a road trip he and his wife took beginning on June 3 from Mattoon east to Pittsburgh, Pennsylvania, and the trials and travails they experienced along the way in this era of dubious road conditions.

The excerpts below illustrate the patience and fortitude the couple had and just some of the situations they encountered.

> *As we started to back down a slight grade a horse hitched to a two-wheeled cart and tied to a post, broke loose and ran away. The way that horse ran would make Barney Oldfield turn green with envy, and he is probably running yet. As this was the first run-away we had ever caused we felt quite grieved about it, and as the citizens who were watching us did not appear overwhelming gracious toward us, we proceeded on our way post haste.*

And the Office Two Hours Away

Perhaps, around the camp-fire, you are hearing that an Indian Wigwam once stood where the Hupmobile is standing—in the fire's glow.

Asphalt pavements, electric lights, social duties, household worries, business cares, the city maelstrom—all mere minutes away in your Hupmobile—the breeze of the night-wrapt woods has blown from your memory.

Coming out this afternoon in your Hupmobile, as you passed successively through

the city traffic, the suburbs, the green farm country and then into the silent, brooding, soothing woods, you felt the shackles of the city's tyranny slipping from you one by one.

About every city—no matter how big, far-flung and grimy—there are still these sacred refuges for troubled minds and jangling nerves. They are there for your week-ends—for you and your children. And the road to Nature's surcease is the car of easy access—The Hupmobile—"The Car of the American Family."

Hupmobile

Hupmobile "32" Touring Car
$1000 f. o. b. Detroit
In Canada, $1180 f. o. b. Windsor

Four-cylinder motor, cylinders 3¼-inch bore by 5½-inch stroke, cast en bloc. Unit power plant.

Selective type transmission, sliding gears.

Irreversible, screw and double nut steering gear.

Full-floating rear axle.

Twelve by two-inch brakes, external contracting and internal expanding.

Wheelbase, 106 inches.

Tires, 32 x 3½ inches.

Equipment of windshield, mohair top with envelope, Jiffy curtains, speedometer, quick detachable rims, rear shock absorber, gas headlights, Prest-O-Lite tank, oil lamps, tools and horn.

Finish, black with nickel trimmings.

"32" Roadster $1000
In Canada, $1160
"32" Six-Passenger . . . $1200
In Canada, $1430
"20" H. P. Runabout . . . $ 750
In Canada, $850
F. O. B. Detroit, or Windsor, fully equipped.

NEXT MONTH
A Hupmobile week-end at the beach

Doubtless you have detected, among Hupmobile owners, a deep-seated feeling of satisfaction and loyalty to the Hupmobile, that falls to the lot of few other cars.

If you have gone further you have probably found, also, good and sufficient reason for this uncommon attitude.

The Hupmobile owner joins in our belief that the Hupmobile is in its class, the best car in the world.

That is why he invested in it.

And its sturdy build, its distinctive features of construction and appearance, its marked economy of operation, its low cost of upkeep—all confirming his belief and ours—only tend to strengthen his conviction and complete his satisfaction.

Hupp Motor Car Company,   1229 Milwaukee Avenue,   Detroit, Michigan
Canadian business handled by Hupp Motor Car Co., Ltd., Factory, Windsor, Ont.

Opposite: Mattoon Motor Car Company advertisement. *Newspapers.com.*

Above: Ad for Hupmobiles sold by Mattoon Motor Car Company. *Author's collection.*

Dr. Iverson Lumpkin and car in later years. *Ben Lumpkin.*

Ernest Tucker and wife on trip east in 1905. *New York Public Library.*

The roads for the first ten miles east of Columbus (Ohio) were a fright, full of chuck holes, hub deep, and full of mud and water at the bottom. It was almost impossible to control the car on this stretch and in trying to avoid a mud hole we got too close to a telephone pole and skidded into it, throwing one front wheel over a small embankment with sufficient force to spring the steering gear rods so much we could not go on.

Two miles west of Cambridge (Ohio) we came to a long arm projecting across the road, the first toll gate either of us ever saw. We produced the necessary silver and passed on to the next one. We passed eight gates in all, through the counties of Guernsey and Belmont, the only two Counties in the state having toll gates.

Having no experience running a car in cities through congested traffic, I was scared to death when we got to the main thoroughfares of Pittsburgh, but through miraculous maneuvering and with the ease of control of the Rambler car, I managed to get through the city without hitting anything or anybody.

View of downtown Pittsburgh around 1905. *Pittsburgh Public Library.*

After journeying about six hundred miles, the couple boarded a train to New York City to continue their eastern tour and shipped their car home to Mattoon by rail. Interestingly, in a nod to equality, the pair shared driving each day so that each could experience "the pleasure of running and also the pleasure of riding without having to pay attention to the driving."[30]

Unfortunately, Tucker died suddenly at the age of forty-nine on February 28, 1927, after an operation for appendicitis.[31]

Although we can only speculate that civic promotion and their love of the road and automobiles led Lumpkin and Tucker to immerse themselves in the Good Roads Movement, fully immerse themselves they did! Though they had some experience organizing a trail association with the Big Four Trail, the Egyptian Trail was a much larger undertaking given the length of the roadway contemplated and the number of towns and counties the road was to pass through. This endeavor was to be a test of their business and organizational acumen.

The exact date that they began formulating plans for the trail is not known, but by the beginning of June 1915, publicity regarding the Egyptian Trail and an organizational meeting to be held in Mattoon on June 15 was appearing in newspapers up and down the proposed route. In addition, city fathers, service garages, auto clubs and merchant and commercial associations were all notified, asking for their support of the proposal and seeking their attendance at the meeting.

Coverage of the meeting from the June 15, 1915 edition of the *Mattoon Journal-Gazette* provides a good summary of the business transacted at it. Highlights from that article follow:

NEW TRAIL IS MAPPED OUT
Egyptian Trail Boosters from Illinois Central Cities Meet Here and Organize

Automobile and good roads enthusiasts along the line of the Illinois Central railroad, at a mass meeting held this afternoon in the Elks club rooms, perfected the organization to be known as the Egyptian Trail, an automobile route that is to be laid out from Chicago to Cairo. Dr. I.A. Lumpkin and Ernest B. Tucker, president and secretary-treasurer of the Big Four Trail, who called today's meeting were chosen unanimously to fill the offices of president and secretary-treasurer of the new organization.

Road conditions near Mattoon around 1915. *IDOT.*

The Egyptian Trail is to have three divisions: Chicago to Paxton, Paxton to Centralia and Centralia to Cairo.

In accordance with a resolution adopted at the meeting, all of the vice-presidents will be required to raise and send to the general secretary-treasurer the sum of $5, to be placed in the expense fund. The raising of the money is to be exclusive of all the funds for other expenses.

The Egyptian Trail is to be blazed with pyramids of orange stamped with the letters E.T. in black. Several suggestions for the trail mark were made. The matter was left finally to a committee of three, consisting of the president, secretary-treasurer and vice-president of Mattoon who acted upon the suggestion of Miss Jessie Akester of Farina, one of the lady enthusiasts at the organization meeting. Miss Akester, at the invitation of President Lumpkin, gracefully expressed her idea as to the form of marker that should be adopted.

Elks Club building in Mattoon. Note antler rack display on third floor of building. *Mattoon Local History Center.*

President Lumpkin and Secretary-Treasurer Tucker expressed their thanks briefly. Dr. Lumpkin said he considered his election as a great honor. He said that he is not engaged in business actively at this time and that the business of the Big Four Trail and the Egyptian Trail will give him something to do.[32]

An article from the front page of the *Centralia Evening Sentinel* on June 17, 1915, fills in some more of the meeting details.

CENTRALIA IS A DIVISION POINT—EGYPTIAN TRAIL
Will Have Meeting in Carbondale Soon to Organize

The Egyptian Trail is organized into three divisions with a general president and secretary-treasurer overall, the latter being Dr. I.A. Lumpkin and E.B. Tucker of Mattoon. Each town is to have its own vice-president. The first division extends from Chicago to Paxton, which has hard roads from Chicago out Halsted Street to Kankakee. The second division from Paxton to Centralia and the third, Centralia to Cairo. The total route has been estimated around 450 miles, it being 315 miles from Centralia to Chicago.

The insignia or mark for the trail is a Centralia suggestion. It being an orange or yellow painted pyramid with the letters E.T. in the center, the pyramid representing the Egyptian idea.

It is planned to mark every other telephone pole with the pyramid mark, and the four poles preceding a turn to each be marked to denote a warning for a turn. Each vice-president along the line is responsible for the marking of the trail and registering his part to halfway to the next located town on the line. This assures the best roads and the most direct route. Each vice president has his town assessed five dollars, he having to furnish the coin or to see that it is raised for the general association expense. Besides this, the vice-president must arrange for his own local expense of marking the poles and doing the routing. This is his voluntary contribution to the cause of good roads and must be done at once.

It is hoped the Goodrich tire people will furnish the mileage marks for the entire route as they have done for other routes, and it is expected to get the entire trail marked at once and the route published in the Blue Book and the official guidebooks of the country in the 1916 editions.[33]

No representatives from Chicago were present at the Mattoon meeting. G.F. Ballou, secretary of the Chicago Automobile Club, sent a letter to Dr. Lumpkin indicating that the Mattoon meeting was too close to the date of Chicago's First 500 Mile International Auto Derby on June 19, which precluded attendance by members of his organization. The race was to be held at the newly constructed Speedway Park in Maywood and was to be put on under the auspices of the club. A streetcar workers' strike actually caused the race to be delayed a week. It was held on June 26 instead. Ballou, however, pledged complete support of his organization to the Egyptian Trail proposal.

William G. Edens, president of the Illinois Highway Improvement Association and the Associated Roads Organization of Chicago and Cook County, also sent a letter to Lumpkin:

> *The Cook County enthusiasts have been having a strenuous campaign on the recent establishment of the Dixie Highway through Illinois and many will be unable to be present tomorrow. Nevertheless, we are in hearty sympathy with your effort to mark the Egyptian Trail from Chicago to Cairo, and in due season I can assure you that the Chicago end of the matter will have full consideration.*

Edens later would figure prominently in the passage of a $60 million road bond issue that would greatly benefit all Egyptian Trail communities.[34]

Despite a lack of attendance by Chicago supporters, the organizational meeting was an unconditional success. Hundreds from across the state turned out to attend, traveling to Mattoon by auto and train. As a result of the meeting, a decision was made to separate the oversight of the trail into three divisions: the southern division to stretch from Cairo to Centralia, the central division to extend from Centralia to Paxton and the northern division to reach from Paxton to downtown Chicago. Further, each division would elect its own president and secretary-treasurer, and each town the trail passed through would appoint a vice-president who would be responsible for helping select the existing, mostly dirt roads to be improved for the route of the trail in their area, raising funds to "blaze" or mark the trail, seeing to it that the roadbed was maintained in good condition and coordinating with adjacent vice-presidents on routing. Plans were also made to ensure each division had its own organizational meeting as soon as possible.

Egyptian Trail mark used to identify route of trail in Illinois. *Author's collection.*

One issue that remained open was what the actual Egyptian Trail mark would look like. Several suggestions were made at the meeting.

MOTOR AGE

When Minutes are Precious

the value of the KLAXON as a time-saver becomes important.

You may wish to meet a train, keep a social engagement, or reach a patient's bedside. Whatever the urgency, you will realize the value of a signal that warns everyone ahead of your approach, and gives time for turning out before you get there.

If you knew that you were alone on a certain road you could "make time" unhampered. With a KLAXON you are not alone, but your half of the road is always ready for you.

Ask your dealer—and send for catalog.

The KLAXONET for small cars has the unusualness of the KLAXON without its harshness. Its tone is a shrill metallic scream about half as loud as the KLAXON. Mechanically it is a reduced copy of the large instrument, and is equally well made and durable.

LOVELL-McCONNELL MFG. CO.
MANUFACTURERS
NEWARK, N. J.

THE KLAXON COMPANY
SOLE DISTRIBUTORS FOR U S A.
1 Madison Avenue, NEW YORK

KLAXON
"The X Ray of Sound"

Advertisement for Klaxon automobile horn. *Author's collection.*

Two of the proposed marks were pyramid-shaped on a yellow or orange background, with the letters "E.T." inside the body of the pyramid in black. A third suggestion was to simply paint alternating bands of brown, black and white on surfaces to signify the route. In July, the matter was settled by the committee charged with selecting a design at the organizational meeting, and trail vice presidents were quickly notified. The route was to be blazed, or marked, by trail signs generally painted on telephone poles, and the official Egyptian Trail mark was to be 12" x 18", painted on poles six feet from the ground. In the center of the sign, a black pyramid was to be painted, flanked by the letter *E* on its left and the letter *T* on its right, both painted in black. The original designs proposed were deemed not to "show well" to motorists and were dropped from consideration.[35]

The *Paxton Record*, in its August 26, 1915 edition, described the background color of the signs as being "a special yellow, or really more of an orange color." This vagueness in description can be attributed to the name of the official background color chosen by the association, which was "Big Four Yellow," manufactured by Lowe Brothers Paint Company of Dayton, Ohio. Though the name implied a yellow color, the actual color shown on company paint chips was unmistakably orange. Lowe Brothers had developed the color for the Cleveland, Cincinnati, Chicago and St. Louis Railroad, also known as the Big Four Railroad, for the rail line's boxcars.[36]

By September 1915, the association was issuing further guidelines for signage and trail marking, chief of which called for signboards to be posted at the entry points of each town indicating the town's name and population and the mileage to the next town.

The association also called for the placement of signs marking dangerous curves, turns, intersections and rail crossings. These signs, worded "Egyptian Trail—Danger—Sound Klaxon," were placed three hundred feet ahead of any danger zone. The Klaxon Company, an early manufacturer of automobile horns, sponsored the signage and likely benefitted from the "advertisements" on the warning signs.[37]

Within just a few months, the Egyptian Trail was well on its way to becoming a reality, and the leaders of the association had worked hard developing standards for all its vice presidents to implement. It was now up to these individuals to get the job done. No time was being lost to get the Egyptian Trail on the map, and it was hoped local trail men would keep up this momentum. The hard part of improving the mostly dirt roads selected to compose the trail was just beginning.

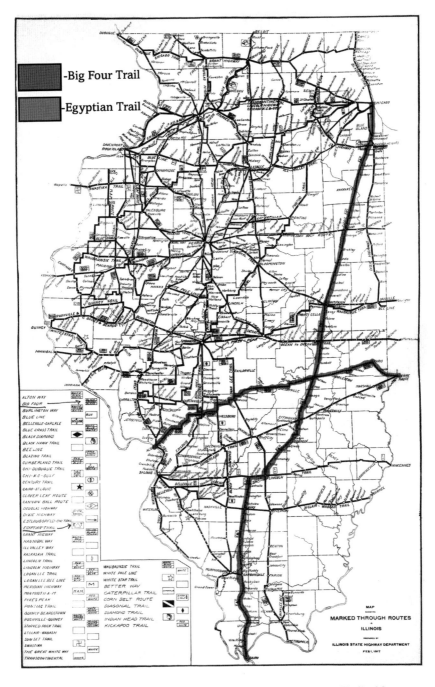

Illinois highway map from 1917 with overlay of Egyptian and Big Four Trails. *Mattoon History Center.*

LITTLE EGYPT

Traditionally, the term Little Egypt refers to the bottom sixteen counties of southern Illinois. The counties of Alexander, Pulaski, Massac, Hardin, Pope, Johnson, Union, Jackson, Williamson, Saline, Gallatin, White, Hamilton, Franklin, Perry and Randolph were considered the strict geographic area that made up Little Egypt. The southernmost city and capitol seat of the district was Cairo, in Alexander County.

The Little Egypt nickname may have resulted from the practices of early settlers from the northern parts of Illinois who traveled to southern Illinois to buy grain after a series of bad winters and droughts. These wagon train folks recognized the similarities between themselves and the ancient Israelites who went to Egypt to buy grain grown in the rich Nile Delta.

A man by the name of Charles Robertson writing in the February 8, 1872 issue of the *Chicago Journal*, seems to support this by telling:

> *Fifty years ago, or in the summer of 1824, there was not a bushel of corn to be found in Central Illinois. My father settled in that year twenty-three miles west of Springfield. We had to live for a time on venison, blackberries, and milk, while the men were gone to "Egypt" to harvest and procure breadstuffs....*
>
> *Thus the southern part of the Illinois, received the appellation of "Egypt" as therein indicated, because, being older, better settled and cultivated, it gathered corn as "the salt of the sea" and the settlers of the central part of the state, after the manner of the children of Israel in their wants, "went to buy and bring from thence that they might live and not die."*

Others say the name Little Egypt came from the early settlers of the region, who thought the area resembled the Nile in Egypt due to the low-lying topography, fertile marshes and flooding from the Mississippi and Ohio Rivers. Thus, both the city of Cairo and the county Alexander were named after the ancient Egyptian places.

Whatever the true explanation is, the term has endured and provided a perfect option for President Lumpkin and Secretary-Treasurer Tucker to name the Egyptian Trail.[38]

Chapter 3

THE NORTHERN DIVISION OF
THE EGYPTIAN TRAIL ASSOCIATION

The Northern Division of the Egyptian Trail Association extended from downtown Chicago south to Paxton, Illinois, a distance of about 110 miles. Motorists travelling the roadway along this route would experience Illinois to the fullest, from the hustle and bustle of traffic and city life in Chicago to the quiet, rural life of the farm communities of north central Illinois. The initial organizational meeting of the northern division was held at the Kankakee County courthouse in Kankakee on July 9, 1915. At that meeting, Charles E. Robinson, Kankakee County treasurer, was selected division president and attorney and president of the Kankakee Commercial Association, and Duane P. Cleghorn was elected secretary-treasurer of the division. Other than selecting the local vice presidents of the towns represented at the meeting, not much else was accomplished. A second meeting was set for September 21, 1915, where specific routing through each town was to be discussed.[39]

Despite a slow organizational start and little of the "boosterism" that may have been present in the southern division's organizing meetings, the people of the northern division were no less enthusiastic about the Egyptian Trail proposal. In fact, they were, and they worked hard to implement the necessary road improvements in their area.

Rather than the mass meetings of boosters that took place in the southern division, northern division organizers held smaller meetings in their own communities to tout the advantages of the Egyptian Trail passing through their towns. This was particularly true for the Cook County towns

Michigan Avenue near the Chicago Art Institute. *Chicago History Museum.*

of Riverdale, Harvey and Homewood. Several meetings were held in each of these towns in September and October 1915, providing citizens with information on the trail and improvements planned for it.[40] These community meetings also had the added emphasis of encouraging Halsted Street to be chosen in the city of Chicago as the route of the Egyptian Trail and through to Riverdale and Harvey. Halsted Street, one of the longest streets in Chicago, was already improved with asphalt paving south through Eighty-Sixth Street at the time. South Cook County organizers felt it was only natural that the street be improved further to the city limits and beyond. The local meetings were also meant to encourage county board representatives to act favorably in this regard.[41]

At these meetings, representatives of the Thornton Township Good Roads Association, the West Pullman and Riverdale Improvement Associations and the Harvey Good Roads Association were present to lend support. In addition to talks by local mayors, the Honorable Frederick DeYoung, Illinois state representative for this district, also attended each and spoke to the good roads issue. Though DeYoung would only serve two

Halsted Street and Seventy-Ninth Street in Chicago. Halsted Street was part of the Egyptian Trail in Chicago. *Chicago History Museum.*

Michigan Avenue looking north toward the Art Institute. *Chicago History Museum.*

terms in the Illinois house, through his "able and persistent efforts," he was instrumental in amending the Tice Law, which made it possible for towns and villages with populations under twenty thousand to benefit from state aid road funding. This was a tremendous boon to smaller communities struggling to fund road projects. In later years, DeYoung served as a justice on the Illinois Supreme Court.

It also did not hurt that two of the biggest proponents of the Egyptian Trail in two of these communities were newspaper editors. Both Albert Lambert of Harvey and Thomas Kinney of Riverdale wrote eloquently about the proposition. In an article for the *Harvey Tribune* on October 15, 1915, Lambert wrote that the Egyptian Trail was

> *a distinctive Illinois project in every way for one end is at Cairo, away down in Egypt, at the extreme southern end of the state and the other end is at Chicago, the metropolis of the state in the north. The building of this great road will do more to encourage the construction of good roads and to pull our fair state out of the mud than any other one thing that can be done, for it will furnish a backbone through the state from which other good roads will radiate and eventually Illinois will not rank twenty-third in the list of states, but first, as a state with modern highways.*

Exaggeration, perhaps, but there was little question that the Egyptian Trail was to be in the vanguard of modern roadways that would span the length and breadth of Illinois, and people like Lambert and Kinney would make it happen.[42]

In Homewood, representatives of the three local country clubs were also present at the village meetings to lend moral and financial support to the Egyptian Trail and having Halsted Street be the preferred route from the city. They felt this path would "furnish the shortest and most direct route to Chicago" from the clubs and pledged themselves to do all they could to help the project along. Better access from the city to their club grounds was good for the clubs and their membership.

The efforts of these men and groups were successful. Halsted Street was selected as the route in Chicago from Fifty-Fifth Street/Garfield Boulevard south to the city limits and through Riverdale and a portion of Harvey. The Cook County board also included portions of this route on its annual appropriation of road improvements for the coming year.[43]

Farther south, in Will County, a "mass meeting" was held in Peotone to discuss good roads and the Egyptian Trail on the evening of October 5,

1915. In announcing the meeting, organizers indicated "every voter in the town of Peotone is invited and encouraged to attend the meeting. The ladies have the same voting privileges on road issues as the men have and they are especially invited to attend." Though women could vote for president in Illinois as early as 1913, it was not until 1920 that they had full voting rights. To make the occasion more festive, the organizers also arranged for Conrad's Military Band and August Schroeder's chorus to render music and song before the start of the meeting. The meeting was a rousing success with well over one hundred voters in attendance, all in support of the Egyptian Trail to "pull Peotone out of the mud and put her on the map."[44]

In Iroquois County, the small town of Buckley was not to be outdone. On Wednesday and Thursday, September 15 and 16, 1915, the town held an Egyptian Trail celebration to boost the roadway. The Paxton Band furnished music on both days, and a ballgame between the Buckley and Paxton baseball teams was held on Wednesday. A parade of "an endless string of automobiles, carriages, phaetons and surreys" was held Thursday as the event, which included "free attractions and amusements," came to a close.[45]

These were some examples of how northern division people did get into the act. At a second meeting of northern division officers at the Kankakee County courthouse on September 21, 1915, Harvey city engineer Arthur Hersey was instructed to draw a map of the northern division route for the local trail vice presidents' approval. Division officers wanted the map completed as quickly as possible so route marking and route improvements could proceed at once.

At the end of the September meeting, William C. Kranz, president of the Kankakee Commercial Association, made a compelling statement to the trail men present, exhorting them to begin their work by saying,

> *Most people traveling from the southern part of Illinois or the middle part of the state for that matter, strike over into Indiana when they want to reach Chicago. These people spend money in the towns through which they pass. These Illinois travelers have taken money out of the state. We will build a road that will make it possible for Illinois people to travel on Illinois roads and spend Illinois money in Illinois cities.*[46]

Kranz recognized that Illinois roads in the northern part of the state were inferior to those in neighboring Indiana, this was hurting economic development in northern communities near the state border and this issue needed to be rectified quickly.

Engineer Hersey got the northern division route map done by early October, and Cook County trail vice presidents were soliciting bids for route marking in November.[47] Joseph Tienstra of Homewood was awarded the contract and had most of the markers in the county done by year's end.[48] Fortunately for painters like Tienstra and others hired to mark the trail, there was very little dispute in towns on the route the Egyptian Trail should take through the northern division. In fact, the only real issue developed from a misinterpretation by the painter marking the trail in Peotone. Instead of marking the route through the town's business district as planned, he marked a route that bypassed it completely. Needless to say, the merchants of Peotone were quite upset and lodged a protest with northern division secretary Cleghorn, who ordered the route remarked immediately.[49]

Though this is not the case today, early roadways were generally directed through local business districts to not only allow "restaurants, ice cream parlors, cigar dealers, dealers in gasoline and garages to profit from the passing tourists who stick to the trail marks like glue" but also to give motorists a greater sense of security through knowing they were near services in case of a malfunction or breakdown in this era when automobiles could be unreliable and required a good deal of maintenance.

By the close of 1915, most northern division communities had begun to make improvements on the trail route through their towns, and more were planned for 1916.

TOWNS OF THE NORTHERN DIVISION OF THE EGYPTIAN TRAIL

Chicago
Cook County, Population 2,701,705 (1920)

Chicago is the second largest city in America as well as the largest railroad center in the world. Thirty-nine railways, including twenty-two great railway systems—(40% of the railway mileage of the U.S.)—terminate in Chicago, in addition to which there are a large number of belt lines, etc., increasing the trackage within the corporate limits. Chicago has more than 10,000 factories and the output of its manufacturing zone is $2,000,000,000 annually. It is the distributing center of the U.S. and *the financial center of the West, the metropolis of the richest agricultural section of the country and the focus of its primary facilities for industrial development, comprising raw materials, transportation, power, labor, factory sites and markets. It is also the largest market for livestock and is the first grain board in the world. Fifty million people live within one night's ride of this great city.*[50]

Post office established: March 31, 1831.

Incorporated: March 4, 1837.

Vice president: William G. Edens, banker.

Route: Jackson Drive and Michigan Avenue, south on Michigan Avenue to Fifty-Fifth Street/Garfield Boulevard (co-alignment with the Dixie Highway), west on Fifty-Fifth Street/Garfield Boulevard to Halsted Street, south on Halsted Street to city limits.[51]

Riverdale
Cook County, Population 1,166 (1920)

Riverdale grew from a site known as Riverdale Crossing, where early settlers George Dolton and J.C. Matthews operated a ferry across the Little Calumet River in the late 1830s. The Illinois Central Railroad came through the area in 1852, and by the 1880s, six other railroads were operating through the town. Early industry included the Charles Pope Beet Sugar Works.

Post office established: February 16, 1874.

Vice president: Thomas F. Kinney, newspaper publisher/editor.

Route: Halsted Street through town.

Sugar beet production was an early agricultural product on the Egyptian Trail. This plant processed the beets into granulated sugar in Riverdale. *Library of Congress.*

Harvey
Cook County, Population 9,216 (1920)

Harvey, first known as South Lawn, was established by Harvey L. Hopkins. The Hopkins Mower Works was the first industry built, in 1880. By 1891, Turlington Harvey had made substantial land purchases in the area and sold this property through the Harvey Land Association for a new "manufacturing" and temperance town. It was said Harvey wanted the town called Turlington, but others suggested Harvey in his honor and for Hopkins.

Post office established: December 13, 1875, as South Lawn; changed to Harvey on March 4, 1890.

Incorporated: 1891.

Vice president: Albert M. Lambert, newspaper publisher/editor.

Route: Halsted Street south to 147th Street, west on 147th Street to Center Avenue, south on Center Avenue to 157th Street, then joining Park Avenue south through the city.

Homewood
Cook County, Population 1,389 (1920)

The Homewood town site was initially platted by James Hart in 1852 and named Hartford. With the arrival of the Illinois Central Railroad in 1853, the depot was named Thornton Station for the existing town of Thornton, three miles east. Thornton Station grew and became the more predominant town. By 1869, residents grew weary of having mail mixed up between Thornton and Thornton Station and petitioned for a name change to Homewood at the suggestion of early resident J.C. Howe.

Post office established: October 3, 1853, as Thornton Station; changed to Homewood on November 15, 1869.

Incorporated: 1893.

Vice president: Dr. James F. Wharton, physician.

Route: Park Avenue south to Dixie Highway, Dixie Highway south through town.

Center Avenue looking south in downtown Harvey toward 154th Street. Center Avenue was part of the Egyptian Trail. *Author's collection.*

The Dixie Highway/Egyptian Trail looking south in Homewood. The Dixie Highway and Egyptian Trail were "co-aligned" through Homewood. Homewood's first traffic signal is pictured. *Author's collection.*

Flossmoor
Cook County, Unincorporated (1920)

In 1891, the Illinois Central Railroad purchased 160 acres of land west of the rail line and north of what is now Flossmoor Road. In the late 1890s, the railroad decided to sell the property for development and sponsored a contest to select a name for the village. "Floss Moor," a Scotch name meaning "dew on the heather" and "gentle rolling countryside," was selected and approved by the U.S. Post Office. Prompted by members of the newly formed Flossmoor Country Club (1899), the railroad built a depot shortly thereafter.

Post office established: February 29, 1904.

Incorporated: 1924.

Vice president: Henry Morgan, insurance.

Route: Dixie Highway south to Illinois Street (Flossmoor Road), west on Illinois Street (Flossmoor Road) to Western Avenue, south on Western Avenue to Lincoln Highway.

Matteson
Cook County, Population 485 (1920)

The Illinois Central Railroad came through the area in 1853, and the town was founded about 1855. It was named after Joel Aldrich Matteson, governor of Illinois from 1853 to 1857.

Post office established: October 3, 1853, as Rich; name changed to Matteson on November 26, 1856.

Incorporated: 1889.

Vice president: Unknown.

Route: Lincoln Highway west to Main Street, south on Main Street to 3rd Street (216th Street), west on 3rd Street (216th Street) to Richton Road, south on Richton Road through town.

Richton
Will County, Unincorporated (1920)

Richton was named by Joseph Batchelder, who settled in the area about 1836–37, for his former home of Richton, Vermont.

View of downtown Matteson showing the route of the Egyptian Trail. *Matteson Historical Society.*

Vice president: John Glaeser.

Route: Richton Road south to Sauk Trail, west on Sauk Trail to road between sections thirty-three and thirty-four (Cicero Avenue), south on Cicero Avenue to Steger Road, west on Steger Road to road between sections four and five—Monee Township (Central Avenue) then south.

Monee
Will County, Population 395 (1920)

The Illinois Central Railroad established a station at Monee in 1853. Augustus Herbert platted the town site that same year. It was named after Marie LeFevre, the part-French, part-Ottawa wife of French trader Joseph Bailly, who was referred to as "Mo-nee" rather than "Ma-rie" in the 1832 Treaty of Tippecanoe. Her descendants were awarded a tract of land in that treaty, which is now part of Monee Township.

Post office established: October 3, 1853.

Incorporated: 1874.

Vice president: John P. Conrad, agricultural implement dealer.

View looking south on Oak Street, a part of the Egyptian Trail, in downtown Monee. *Monee Historical Society.*

Route: South from Monee Township line on road between sections 4 and 5 (Central Avenue) to Fred Deutsche's corner (Main Street), east on First North Street (Main Street), cross railroad and then south on Oak Street through town.

Peotone
Will County, Population 1,090 (1920)

Peotone was established by the Illinois Central Railroad when its depot was built in 1856. The name Peotone is believed to be derived from a Potawatomi word meaning "bring" or "come here." An alternate version indicates that the town was named for a Native American chief; in yet another variation of the story, an Illinois Central official came up with the name by "combining consonant and vowels chosen at random, as he made his first trip of inspection down the line."[52]

Post office established: June 10, 1857.

Incorporated: 1869.

Vice president: John P.F. Conrad, grocer.

Route: South from Monee to Lawler's Corner (Eagle Lake Road), west one mile to the Peterson School (Ridgeland Avenue), south two miles to the Barton School (Beecher-Peotone Road), east one mile to the town line, then

View looking east on Main Street toward Second Street, both part of the Egyptian Trail in Peotone. *Author's collection.*

west on Crawford Street to Second Street, south on Second Street to Main Street, west on Main Street to First Street, south on First Street to Corning Road, west on Corning Road to the Loomis corner (Rathje Road), south for one and a half miles to the Piper School (Kennedy Road), west two miles to Standard School (Center Road), then south one mile to Henry Piper's corner at the county line.

Manteno
Kankakee County, Population 1,182 (1920)

The name Manteno was derived from that of the Potawatomi maiden Mawteno, granddaughter of Francois Bourbonnais Sr. and his wife, Catish. Both Mawteno and Catish received land in the Treaty of *Tippecanoe* in 1832, land that was absorbed into Kankakee County as the Illinois Central Railroad was building and naming sites for its depots. Manteno was originally called Manteno Depot, in 1853.

Post office established: April 25, 1854.
Incorporated: 1878.
Vice president: Otto Weber, grocer.
Route: Unknown.

Bourbonnais
Kankakee County, Population 620 (1920)

The village was named for François Bourbonnais Sr., a fur trapper, hunter and agent of John Jacob Astor's American Fur Company, who married a Native American woman and arrived in the area near the fork of two major Indian trails and the Kankakee River around 1830. Two years later, Noel LeVasseur and Gurdon Hubbard, both traders, arrived. LeVasseur, born in the province of Quebec, located his fur trading post in Bourbonnais Grove and became the first permanent non–Native American settler of the area.

Post office established: May 6, 1836, initially as Kankakee; name changed to Bulbona's Grove on March 15, 1838, then to Bourbonnais Grove on June 30, 1855, and finally to Bourbonnais on June 20, 1892.

Vice president: None.

Route: Unknown.

Kankakee
Kankakee County, Population 16,753 (1920)

Kankakee, situated on the Kankakee River, is famous for the natural beauty of its scenery. The Kankakee State Hospital, largest of its kind in the world, is located here. The area was first explored by LaSalle for France in 1680. Native Americans called the river Teakiki or Thiakiki, among other spellings, which may have meant "swampy ground" or "open, exposed country." The French corrupted the name to Kiakiki and eventually Kankakee. The town developed after the Illinois Central Railroad bypassed the already established village of Bourbonnais and built a depot in Kankakee in 1853. The first train passed through on July 4, 1853.

Post office established: October 3, 1853, as Kankakee Depot; named changed to Kankakee on June 7, 1866.

Vice president: Wallis R. Sanborn, quarry owner

Route: Schuyler Avenue south to River Street, west on River Street to Washington Avenue, south on Washington Avenue across bridge, jog west at Charles Street, then south on Washington Avenue to Jeffery Street, east on Jeffery Street to Kensington Avenue and south on Kensington Avenue out of the city.[53]

Kankakee County Fairgrounds along the Egyptian Trail in the city of Kankakee. *Kankakee County Historical Museum.*

Chebanse
Kankakee/Iroquois Counties, Population 541 (1920)

Chebanse was established as a stop on the Illinois Central Railroad in 1854 and named for Chebanse or Chebass (Little Duck), a Potawatomi chief who was signatory to the Treaty of Chicago in 1821.

Post office established: June 15, 1855.

Vice president: F.J. Hennessey, banker.

Route: At Otto Township line, south on road between sections 27 and 26 (2000 West Road) four and a half miles, then jog east across the Illinois Central Railroad (7000 South Road), then south to Oak Street through town.

Clifton
Iroquois County, Population 638 (1920)

Clifton developed with the construction of the Illinois Central Railroad in the area in 1854. It was named by William A. Veech, an early landowner, for the Clifton House, a hotel in Chicago where he had previously boarded.

Post office established: August 24, 1857.

Vice president: William C. Hobson, butcher.

Route: Main Street through town.

Ashkum
Iroquois County, Population 638 (1920)

Ashkum was founded in 1856 along the Illinois Central Railroad. The town was named for a Potawatomi leader whose name appears in a number of treaties in the 1820s and 1830s. His name reportedly meant "more and more."

Post office established: June 24, 1856.

Vice president: Richard R. Meents, banker.

Route: Front Street through town.

Danforth
Iroquois County, Population 398 (1920)

Danforth's beginnings date to about 1854, when A.H. and George W. Danforth began purchasing land in the area following construction of the Illinois Central Railroad. The town site was laid out in 1872.

Post office established: January 11, 1866, as Danforth Station; name changed to Danforth on May 21, 1883.

Vice president: John Kuipers, farmer.

Route: Central Street through town.

Gilman
Iroquois County, Population 1,448 (1920)

Gilman was laid out in 1857 on land where the Peoria and Oquawka Railroad—later the Toledo, Peoria and Western Railway—would cross the

Illinois Central Railroad. It was named for Samuel Gilman, a partner in the firm Cruger, Secor and Company, which oversaw the construction of the Peoria and Oquawka Railroad between Gilman and El Paso, Illinois.

Post office established: March 2, 1858, as Douglas City; name changed to Gilman on July 13, 1858.

Vice president: Unknown.

Route: From the north through Douglas Township, south to Mrs. Frey's corner (North 800 East Road & County Road 1900 North), then west (CR 1900 North) to the corner just south of Wegner Cemetery (CR 1900 North & CR 750 East), south (CR 750 East) to Second Street, then west on Second Street to the Onarga Road (600 East Road), then south on the Onarga Road (600 East Road) out of town.

Onarga
Iroquois County, Population 1,302 (1920)

Onarga was laid out in 1854 by David A. Neal, vice president of the Illinois Central Railroad. Its name may be of Native American origin, meaning "a place of rocky hills," but this is uncertain. The town was home to the Grand Prairie Seminary, a coeducational private "preparatory" school, established in 1863, which became the Onarga Military School in 1917.

Post office established: March 24, 1854, as Onargo; name changed to Onarga on December 31, 1869.

Vice president: Melvin T. Ammerman, grocer/general store owner.

Route: School Street (Evergreen Street) through town.

Preparation work for brick pavement in downtown Onarga. *Onarga Historical Society.*

Buckley
Iroquois County, Population 461 (1920)

Buckley was founded in 1856 by Ira A. Manly, the first station agent for the Illinois Central Railroad assigned there. Manly named it either for a Philadelphia relative named Bulkley or for an employee of the Illinois Central.

Post office established: June 2, 1858, as Bulkley; changed to Buckley on August 25, 1865.

Vice president: Thomas H. Fencken, grocer.

Route: Railroad Avenue through town.

Loda
Iroquois County, Population 530 (1920)

Loda was established as a station by the Illinois Central Railroad in 1855. The origin of the name is uncertain. Some sources indicate it is a Native American woman's name meaning "light of the woods"; others suggest it was the name of an Illinois Central employee's wife or that it may have been taken from the epic poem legendary Irish hero Ossian, "Cath-loda," by Scottish poet James MacPherson.

Loda's business district. *Author's collection.*

Post office established: November 9, 1855, as Mixville; name changed to Okalla on December 21, 1855, and then changed to Loda on March 10, 1880.

Vice president: Frank Butzow, banker.

Route: Oak Street through town.

Chicago's Motor Row

This group of commercial buildings on Chicago's near South Side, stretching from just south of Roosevelt Road to Twenty-Sixth Street on Michigan Avenue, is considered to be the largest intact early "automobile row" in the United States. Auto rows developed in numerous cities shortly after 1900 as car companies sought to create districts where the sale and repair of cars could become an easy urban shopping experience.

At its peak, as many as 116 different makes of automobiles were being sold on Chicago's Motor Row. Some are familiar today, including Ford,

Auburn, Cord, Duesenberg showroom on Chicago Motor Row. *Chicago History Museum.*

Buick, Fiat and Cadillac, while others are better known to historians and old-car buffs, including Hudson, Locomobile, Marmon and Pierce-Arrow. Motorists traveling into Chicago along the Egyptian Trail would pass by these dealerships, as Michigan Avenue was part of the trail route in Chicago.

The range of buildings in Motor Row illustrates the evolution of the automobile showroom and related product and service buildings, from simple two-story structures used for display and offices to multistory buildings housing a variety of departments for the repair, storage, painting and finishing of automobiles. The district was built between 1905 and 1936, and many of these buildings were designed by noted architects, including Holabird & Roche, Alfred Alschuler, Christian Eckstorm, Philip Maher and Albert Kahn.

The Motor Row District was designated a Chicago Landmark on December 13, 2000, and some of the buildings have been or are being redeveloped into condominiums, nightclubs and retail storefronts.[54]

Chapter 4

THE CENTRAL DIVISION OF THE EGYPTIAN TRAIL ASSOCIATION

T he central division of the Egyptian Trail traveled from Paxton to Centralia, a distance of about 163 miles, through the corn and soybean belt of Illinois. Minerals deposited by glaciers and subsequent prairie growth for thousands of years blessed this region and central Illinois with some of the world's most fertile topsoil. In addition to being the agricultural engine of the state, the central division was also home to the state's premier institution of higher learning, the University of Illinois at Urbana-Champaign, and one lesser-known institution of higher learning, the Illinois College of Photography and Photoengraving at Effingham. Manufacturing in the cities of Mattoon and Effingham rounded out the economic activity of the division.

Since representatives were present from most of the towns comprising the division at the general organizing meeting for the Egyptian Trail held in Mattoon on June 15, 1915, they wasted no time and held an organizational meeting for the central division that same afternoon. At this meeting, Frank M. Schulhoff, a successful retail merchant from Mattoon, was named division president, and Dwight M. Morris, a salesman from Salem, was elected division secretary-treasurer. Other business at the meeting included the selection of the local vice presidents for the central division towns.[55]

The original plan was to have the city of Champaign serve as the southern terminal point for the northern division of the Egyptian Trail and the northern terminal point for the central division. At the June 15 meeting in Mattoon, Paxton representative Gustaf L. Johnson pushed for his city to have these honors. Johnson was able to convince those at the meeting that Paxton was the most logical terminal for the north and central divisions, being a little over one hundred miles south of Chicago, and that the town benefited from good roads leading east and west in and out of it. Paxton was selected, but this was likely due to the fact there were no representatives from Champaign at the meeting to rebut his contentions. In fact, Champaign was essentially equidistant from Chicago and Centralia, between 135 and 150 miles from each.[56]

A routing issue was another matter that was settled at the first meeting of the central division. Automobile and good roads boosters from Salem in Marion County with state senator Charles E. Hull as their spokesman came to Mattoon in four automobiles and reported good roads all the way to within one mile of Mattoon. While Salem was not on the Illinois Central Railroad, the boosters from there put up a "good argument" as to why their town should be included on the route of the Egyptian Trail. The delegation from Salem assured those at the meeting that the route would be much better and no longer than that along the railroad. They also stated that the city had good garage facilities and good hotels that would be drawing cards to automobile tourists. Although Senator Hull said he and his colleagues had come to the meeting unbidden, Salem was eager to have a spot on the trail. His arguments were convincing, and Salem became an Egyptian Trail community with Senator Hull as its local vice president. From Salem, the route was to travel west through the town of Odin and then to Sandoval and south to Centralia.[57]

A second meeting of the central division vice presidents was held in Mattoon on July 7, 1915, and nineteen of the twenty-one trail vice presidents were present. At this meeting, Sandoval was accepted as an Egyptian Trail community, the trail men adopted a detailed route of the road from Paxton to Centralia and with general president Dr. Lumpkin and general secretary-treasurer Tucker present, the official mark or emblem of the Egyptian Trail was adopted.[58]

There were few routing disputes in the central division, likely given the flat topography of the division, which posed little impediment to smooth travel. One issue did develop over whether the trail would pass through Urbana or Champaign, though it was not much of a dispute and Charles A. Kiler, the local vice president for Champaign, laid the issue to rest quickly. He proclaimed the trail was to pass through Champaign—and furthermore, it was to go down Neil Street, the street where the furniture store he owned was located.

Central division vice presidents were quick to work to drag, grade and otherwise improve the roads selected to form the highway. Other citizens volunteered in different ways. Paul Ramser, a farmer from the Marion

County town of Alma, made a welcome offer of one hundred railcar loads of gravel from a gravel pit he owned near the Alexander County town of Tamms, a few miles west of the proposed route of the trail in the southern division. The only cost involved would be transportation expenses to the sites where the gravel would be needed.[59]

In addition to overseeing the work on the trail near his hometown of Farina, local vice president and lumber and grain merchant Charles T. Wade took promotion of the Egyptian Trail even a step further. Shortly after the trail route was proposed, he started construction of a fine brick service garage building in Farina and named it the Egyptian Trail Garage. It opened for business in September 1915, and the local newspaper also moved its offices into a space on the south end of the building.[60] It was likely the first business along the route to take the Egyptian Trail name—but not the last. In Champaign, in the fall of 1915, the Egyptian Trail Motorcycle Garage opened at 511 South Neil Street. The business was a dealer for Pope and Indian motorcycles and serviced other makes, as well.[61]

Later, another business, the Egyptian Trail Oil Station in the northern division town of Onarga, took the trail's name. In addition to the service station, there was a lunch stand on the premises, and Ed Farr, the owner, had added an unusual attraction. In the mid-1920s, he "imported" alligators from Florida, which he displayed in a tank along the roadside to entice motorists to stop at his businesses.[62]

A sign of how quickly the initial work proceeded in the central division was reported by the *Paxton Record* in its August 26, 1915 edition. The paper

Egyptian Trail Garage in Farina, one of the first businesses to use the Egyptian Trail name. *Rick Switzer.*

Advertisement for Egyptian Trail Motorcycle Garage in Champaign. *Newspapers.com.*

Egyptian Trail Oil Station in Onarga. *Onarga Historical Society.*

reported that "F.L. Zilske, painter for the Egyptian Trail, arrived in Paxton Monday afternoon at 3 o'clock, having covered the distance from Cairo to this city in six weeks, in which he painted the trail emblem on every other telephone pole." The paper further indicated that the last emblem painted was the one located on the newspaper's bulletin board in front of the Paxton Hotel.[63]

As 1915 came to a close, central division communities were well pleased with the Egyptian Trail and the work completed on it to date.

Towns of the Central Division of the Egyptian Trail

Paxton
Ford County, Population 3,033 (1920)

Paxton was originally called Prairie City and then Prospect City by an Illinois Central Railroad official in 1855. The name was changed to Paxton in 1859 for Sir Joseph Paxton. Paxton was a noted English architect and horticulturalist and a major shareholder in the Illinois Central who was interested in organizing an English settlement in the state.

Post office established: October 6, 1854, as Ten Mile Grove; changed to Prospect City on January 14, 1857, and then to Paxton on September 15, 1859.

Vice president: Gustaf J. Johnson, jeweler.

Route: Unknown.

Ludlow
Champaign County, Population 343 (1920)

Ludlow was originally known as Pera or Pera Station, a stop on the Illinois Central Railroad. In 1867, the name was changed for Thomas W. Ludlow, one of the incorporators and major shareholders of the railroad.

Post office established: December 22, 1854, as Pera Station; name changed to Ludlow on March 8, 1867.

Vice president: Louis N. Bear, general store merchant.

Route: Unknown.

2150. BIRD'S EYE VIEW OF AVIATION FIELD SHOWING. HANGARS.

CHANUTE AVIATION FIELD, RANTOUL, ILLINOIS

Chanute Air Force Base in Rantoul was active from 1917 to 1993. *Author's collection.*

Rantoul
Champaign County, Population 1,551 (1920)

Rantoul was laid out in 1854 for the Illinois Central Railroad and named after Robert Rantoul Jr., a stockholder and director of the railroad. Rantoul was also a United States representative from Massachusetts who went on to fill the unexpired term of Daniel Webster in the U.S. Senate. The town of Rantoul was home to Chanute Field, an army air base, established on May 21, 1917. The area was previously known as Mink Grove.

Post office established: August 1, 1856, as Rantoul Station; name changed to Rantoul on May 9, 1862.

Vice president: James Clark, attorney.

Route: Unknown.

Thomasboro
Champaign County, Population 261 (1920)

Thomasboro was founded in 1864 along the Illinois Central by Englishman and early landowner John Thomas.

Post office established: March 7, 1865, as Thomasborough; name changed to Thomasboro on October 14, 1893.

Vice president: Charles E. Kelso, general store merchant.

Route: Unknown.

Champaign
Champaign County, Population 15,873 (1920)

Champaign County dates to 1833, when Illinois state senator John Vance introduced legislation creating a new county. A native of Urbana, Champaign County, Ohio, he chose the name Champaign for the new Illinois county and the name Urbana for its county seat. The city of Champaign was platted in 1853, originally as West Urbana. The name was changed to Champaign in 1860. Champaign and Urbana are known as the Twin Cities of Illinois and are home to the University of Illinois, the state's great educational institution of higher learning.

Post office established: March 2, 1855, as West Urbana; name changed to Champaign on April 28, 1860.

View looking south on Neil Street, a part of the Egyptian Trail in Champaign. *Urbana Free Library.*

Vice president: Charles A. Kiler, furniture store merchant.

Route: Market Street south to Washington Street, west on Washington Street to Neil Street, then south through town on Neil Street.

Tolono
Champaign County, Population 693 (1920)

Tolono was founded in 1856 by the Illinois Central Railroad. There are several versions of how the town got its name. The two most plausible claim that the Illinois Central purchased land in the area from men whose names were Todd, Logan and Noyes, and a requirement of the sale was that the first parts of the men's names were to be used to name the town. The other version is that early Illinois Central land agent J.B. Calhoun created the name simply by "placing the vowel *o* three times, thus o-o-o, and filling in with the consonants t-l-n, forming Tolono."[64]

Post office established: June 8, 1857.

Vice president: Unknown.

Route: Unknown.

Pesotum
Champaign County, Population 478 (1920)

Pesotum was established by the Illinois Central in 1854. It was named for Pesotum, a Potawatomi leader whose main village was near Lake Michigan and who is believed to have killed Captain William Wells in the Fort Dearborn massacre on August 15, 1812.

Post office established: June 24, 1856.

Vice president: Julius A. Heinz, banker/undertaker.

Route: Chestnut Street through town.

Tuscola
Douglas County, Population 2,564 (1920)

Tuscola was established by the Illinois Central in 1855. The name is likely Native American in origin. The Choctaw word *tashka* or *tushka* means "warrior"; *ola* means "sound" or "many sounds." Hence, the name Tuscola

Main Street in Tuscola, a part of the Egyptian Trail. *Douglas County Museum.*

could literally be taken to mean "warrior's cry." A more liberal interpretation might be "warrior people." Another source feels the name Tuscola means "warrior prairie."

Post office established: December 13, 1857.[65]

Vice president: Albert W. Wallace, banker.

Route: South on Main Street to Scott Street, east on Scott Street to Niles Avenue, south on Niles Avenue, thence south on the Arcola Road. Main Street was also part of the Pikes Peak Ocean to Ocean Highway.[66]

Arcola
Douglas County, Population 1,831 (1920)

Arcola was established by the Illinois Central Railroad as Okaw in 1855. So as not to be confused with a similarly named town in another county, its name was changed to Arcola. Some sources indicate the town was named for the village of Arcole in northern Italy, where Napoleon defeated the Austrians in 1796. Others indicate the name was suggested by James Kearney to the Illinois Central station agent, perhaps in homage to one of the many towns named Arcola in eastern states. The region was the center of broomcorn production in the nineteenth and early twentieth centuries.

Post office established: July 23, 1857.

An early view of Main Street in Arcola, a part of the Egyptian Trail. *Douglas County Museum.*

Vice president: James H. Davidson, road commissioner.

Route: South on Elm Street to Main Street, west on Main Street to end of road and then south (now CR 800 East).

Humboldt
Coles County, Population 343 (1920)

Humboldt was first called Milton in 1859, so named for a local businessman. Its name was changed to Humboldt in 1860 at the suggestion of the postmaster, an admirer of German traveler and naturalist Friedrich Heinrich Alexander von Humboldt, who had died a year earlier. The town's name was initially recorded as Humbolt.

Post office established: March 16, 1858, as Milton Station; name changed to Humbolt on June 25, 1875, and then to Humboldt on June 20, 1892.

Vice president: F.H. Pardleck, farmer.

Route: Broadway Street through town.

Mattoon
Coles County, Population 13,552 (1920)

Mattoon is a beautiful little city of about 15000 population, which takes pride in its many miles of fine wide streets and well-kept boulevards. It has excellent railroad facilities, and this combined with its unlimited water supply and cheap power makes it well adapted to manufacturing industries. It is at the center of the great broom corn belt of central Illinois and among its manufactories are broom and tile factories, railway repair shops, foundries, etc.[67]

Post office established: July 14, 1855.
Incorporated: February 22, 1859.
Vice president: George W. Byers, hotel owner.
Route: South on Tenth Street to Broadway, west to Eighteenth Street and then south through town.

Broadway Avenue looking east near the rail depot in Mattoon. *Author's collection.*

Business district view of west side of rail tracks in Neoga. *Neoga Public Library.*

Neoga
Cumberland County, Population 1,149 (1920)

Neoga was established by the Illinois Central Railroad in 1854. The origin of the name is uncertain; one source suggests that it was created from the Iroquois words *neo* (deity) and *oga* (place)—thus, "place of the deity"— while another indicates that the name may have come from the Seneca or Kickapoo word for *deer*.

Post office established: May 7, 1852, as Long Point Grove; name changed to Neoga on January 7, 1857.

Vice president: Abraham L. Woolery, farmer/livestock dealer.

Route: Oak Avenue through town.

Sigel
Shelby County, Population 292 (1920)

Sigel was established along the Illinois Central by Theodore Hoffman in 1863. It was named after Franz Sigel, a German soldier who emigrated to the United States and joined the Union army in 1861. He rose to the rank of major general.

Post office established: April 22, 1863, as Hooker; name changed to Sigel on June 27, 1871.

Vice president: Alexander W. Bigler—hay/grain merchant.

Route: Unknown.

Effingham
Effingham County, Population 4,024 (1920)

Effingham is a manufacturing city surrounded by a fine agricultural and dairy district. Two of the principal industries are Van Camp Packing Company and the Mullen, Blackledge & Nellis Company. It also enjoys the distinction of having the Illinois College of Photography and the Illinois College of Photo-Engraving, the only institutions of their kind in the world, attracting students from all over the globe.[68]

Incorporated: February 20, 1861.

Vice president: Lewis H. Bissell, owner, Illinois College of Photography

Route: South on Fourth Street to Jefferson Street, then west to Fifth Street, then south through town on Fifth Street.

Benwood Hotel in Effingham, an early luxurious hotel along the Egyptian Trail route. *Author's collection.*

Watson
Effingham County, Population 316 (1920)

Watson was established in 1856 and named for George Watson, a division superintendent for the Illinois Central Railroad.

Post office established: January 13, 1859, as Salt Creek; name changed to Watson on October 7, 1868.

Vice president: Arthur L. Abrams, general store merchant.

Route: Unknown.

Mason
Effingham County, Population 324 (1920)

Mason was first known as Bristol and later Clio. When the Illinois Central Railroad was completed in 1853, the town site was moved north to align with the tracks. The depot was named after Colonel Roswell B. Mason, chief engineer for the railroad, who subsequently became mayor of the city of Chicago and was mayor during the Great Chicago Fire.

Post office established: March 31, 1852, as Ione; name changed to Mason on August 5, 1857.

Vice president: Aden K. Gibson, banker.

Route: Unknown.

Edgewood
Effingham County, Population 438 (1920)

Edgewood was laid out in 1857 by A.J. Galloway for the Illinois Central Railroad. The name likely comes from one of over one hundred Edgewoods in the eastern states at the time.

Post office established: March 23, 1858.

Vice president: William Faulk, postmaster.

Route: Unknown.

Downtown scene in Farina. *Author's collection.*

Farina
Fayette County, Population 701 (1920)

Farina was founded in 1857 along the Illinois Central and was named for the station, which is believed to have been named Farina, Latin for "flour," because it was situated in a wheat-growing region.

Post office established: September 22, 1858.

Vice president: Charles T. Wade, lumber/grain merchant

Route: Chestnut Street through town.

Kinmundy
Marion County, Population 898 (1920)

Kinmundy was laid out along the Illinois Central Railroad by William T. Sprouse and named for the birthplace in Scotland of William Ferguson, a member of the British firm of Robert Benson & Company, Illinois Central stockholders. Ferguson visited the area in 1856 and wrote a book on his American travels.

Post office established: July 14, 1855.

Vice president: Frank C. Hensley, grocery store merchant

Route: Unknown.

Alma
Marion County, Population 366 (1920)

Alma was laid out by John S. Martin along the Illinois Central in 1854. Its name was suggested in 1855 by John B. Calhoun, a land agent for the railroad, to commemorate the Alma River in Crimea, where the allied French and British army defeated the Russians in a battle fought on September 20, 1854.

Post office established: April 13, 1855.

Vice president: T.E. Maulding, general store merchant.

Route: Railroad Street through town.

Salem
Marion County, Population 3,457 (1920)

Salem, the county seat of Marion County, was settled as early as 1811, and the town was laid out in 1823. It was primarily an agricultural community until oil was discovered, which fueled a boom in economic growth. Salem is also the birthplace of William Jennings Bryan, a three-time candidate for U.S. president. His family home is maintained as a museum.

Post office established: May 3, 1825.[69]

Vice president: Charles E. Hull, senator and grocery store/dry goods merchant.

Route: Main Street through town.

William Jennings Bryan home, a local tourist attraction, in Salem. *Author's collection.*

Odin
Marion County, Population 1,385 (1920)

Odin was founded by the Illinois Central Railroad about 1856. Since many early settlers were Scandinavian, the town was named after Odin, the god of war, learning and poetry in Scandinavian mythology.
Post office established: February 15, 1858.
Vice president: Horace N. Woodward, general store merchant.
Route: Poplar Street through town.

Sandoval
Marion County, Population 1,768 (1920)

Sandoval was established on the Illinois Central Railroad, and a survey was made for the city in May 1855. Its name is of uncertain origin but believed to be that of an old Mexican or Spanish chief. The town was a crossing on the Illinois Central and the Ohio and Mississippi Railroad, which later became a part of the Baltimore and Ohio Railroad. Its early industries included coal mining, smelting, oil, strawberries and tomato canning.
Post office established: December 22, 1854.[70]
Vice president: Fish Wilson.
Route: Unknown.

AUTOMOBILE ROUTE GUIDES AND ROAD MAPS

When the start of the twentieth century brought the automobile, it soon became evident that the existing bicycle and railroad maps would not serve well for this new form of transportation. Color overprints of auto roads on these maps caused cartographic confusion. A better method of mapping the road was needed. The very first auto guides provided extensive descriptions in text form only. The guidebooks gave specific turn-by-turn instructions, generally referencing mileage and landmarks the driver should watch for while following them. Even a simple trip required reading a book, which generally meant a "co-pilot" was needed. Day travel was the norm under these circumstances, and driving solo would be difficult while trying to read the instructions in these books, which sometimes could be two inches thick.

Left: Clason Map Company guidebook. *Author's collection.*

Right: Rand McNally Auto Trails Map book. *Author's collection.*

In addition to making sure the auto was well maintained for any trip, a well-calibrated speedometer was a necessity to ensure that instructions were properly followed. Driving could be a nerve-racking and exhausting ordeal, what with following the instructions, monitoring mileage and constantly being on the lookout for landmarks. And this was the case when all went well; missed turns posed more headaches!

Some of the earliest and popular versions of these guides were *The Official Automobile Blue Book*, published by the Automobile Blue Book Publishing Company for the American Automobile Association; *The Automobile Green Book*, published by the Scarborough Motor Guide Company; and *King's Official Route Guide*.

This cumbersome format was soon replaced by smaller and more practical guides with strip maps of principal routes, keyed to descriptions

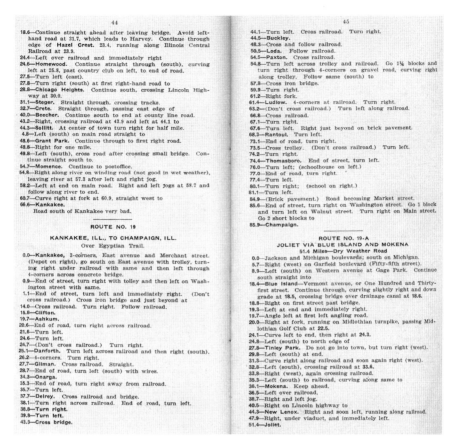

Sample automobile trail guidebook page. *Author's collection.*

of hotels, gas stations, mechanics and other locations essential for the early auto traveler. Well-known artists were commissioned to do the vivid cover graphics. These guides and the later familiar road atlas were produced by companies like Rand McNally and the Clason Map Company.

Illinois produced its first official road map in 1917. This map and other earlier versions were not detailed enough to provide specific driving instructions. It was not until 1924 that state maps developed that detail, allowing for drivers to easily navigate from town to town in Illinois. Soon, oil companies were distributing road maps at their service stations, and these maps became a staple in the American automobile for the rest of the century.

Today, with GPS navigation systems in cars, auto maps have fast become a quaint relic of the past.

Chapter 5

THE SOUTHERN DIVISION OF
THE EGYPTIAN TRAIL ASSOCIATION

T he Southern Division of the Egyptian Trail stretched from Centralia to Cairo, through the heart of "Little Egypt" in the far reaches of southern Illinois. An organizational meeting for the division was held on June 24, 1915, in the opera house at Carbondale. By all accounts, the meeting was the most enthusiastic held for the Egyptian Trail proposition. In fact, it was scheduled to be held in the Carbondale city hall, but organizers anticipated attendance would be great and held it in the opera house instead. Even there, it was standing room only, and some boosters were still unable to get in. Attendance was estimated at over 550 persons.[71]

The *Centralia Evening Sentinel* covered the meeting in great detail, and an article published on the newspaper's front page on June 25, 1915, gives interesting information on the proceedings.

Carbondale Meet Was Great Boost for Good Roads

The meeting at Carbondale played to a full house, even the fire escape had to be let down to handle the crowd in getting in. The meeting was unquestionably the biggest testimonial to good roads interest which southern Illinois has ever witnessed. Towns along the line had trail signs up and everywhere it was noted interest was keen. Carbondale sent about forty autos on their five miles of hard road out to meet the coming of the machines from the north. The crowd had a band with them and a big parade of about one hundred autos followed into town. The full band was also out, furnishing music on the streets, and Carbondale did herself proud in entertaining the visitors from the north and south.

The meeting did not get down to business until after two o'clock, the crowd being held to wait for Anna, Cairo and towns down the line which came in on the 1:52 train, it having rained south and prevented a crowd coming up in machines. John W. Miller, a prominent lumberman of Carbondale called the meeting to order, and was later elected temporary and then permanent president for the southern division. The mayor of Carbondale gave an address of welcome and then Chairman Miller introduced Dr. I.A Lumpkin, association general president and "daddy" of the Egyptian Trail movement. The doctor gave a short talk detailing the preliminary movement; had general secretary Tucker read the Mattoon minutes which supported his contention that he could not rightfully recognize the opposition movement from Salem, Mt. Vernon, Benton, and Vienna. He then recognized W.E. Joy of Centralia for a resolution which called for the election of vice-presidents from the towns and villages along the Illinois Central Railroad, as per the original call and orders of the meeting at Mattoon on June 15th. The resolution was seconded by DuQuoin and went through with a roof raising whoop as those present realized it settled the fight and ended the agony as to the location of the trail from Centralia to Cairo.

G.W. Schwartz of Carbondale, secretary of the retail merchant's association there and another "live wire" was made permanent secretary for the southern division, it being the custom to elect the president and secretary from the same city to facilitate business when organizing trail movements.[72]

The article alludes to a routing dispute that had developed at the Mattoon meeting on June 15, 1915, which was the first test of the association's philosophy and Dr. Lumpkin's authority as president. At that meeting, a delegation from the city of Mt. Vernon was present to lobby for a spot on the trail traveling south to Cairo on a route farther east of what had been originally proposed. The Mt. Vernon representative who spoke on their behalf told how this option provided "a broad, level highway with all concrete bridges and a road surface with speed possibilities of forty-five miles per hour from Kinmundy to Cairo on the natural or dividing watershed between the Mississippi and Ohio Rivers, such a road leading through Mt. Vernon."

Reports from the day indicated that

those travelers who made part of the route Kirby Smith of Mt. Vernon discussed, sat with open mouth, stupefied as they listened to the gentlemen's eloquence. Then as the spell was over, the gaping Egyptians slowly closed their mouths and broadened into a knowing smile as they looked to each other

and remarked "whatdoyouknowaboutthat." The gentlemen's eloquence is to
be complimented but the facts and his eloquence were total strangers, as anyone
knows who has tried to motor the Ozark remnants his route proposes.[73]

It appears that the roadway put forth by Mt. Vernon was not only in poor
condition, but it was also not a route that followed as directly as possible
the Illinois Central Railroad, one of the original requisites for a roadway
to be included in the Egyptian Trail Association. A motion was made at
that meeting that the route follow the original plan as best as possible and
proceed through the town of Salem to Centralia. The motion passed, but
the Mt. Vernon folks were not satisfied. There was intelligence received that
Mt. Vernon would again try to address its route proposal at the Carbondale
meeting. On hearing of this, Dr. Lumpkin feared it would derail the agenda
for the meeting, which was set to discuss specific routing and improvements
through the approved towns. The day before the Carbondale meeting was to
take place, he contacted the Mt. Vernon representatives and advised that he
could not and would not entertain any motion to the contrary at the meeting.
He further advised it would be "a waste of time" to come to Carbondale. He
must have been persuasive, as no one from Mt. Vernon or the towns south of
it showed up in Carbondale. This matter was solved.

Undeterred, Kirby Smith and the Mt. Vernon contingent ended up
establishing the Logan-Lee Highway Association, which worked to create an
improved roadway running from Paducah, Kentucky, through Mt. Vernon,
Springfield, Peoria and on to Rock Island, Illinois.[74]

The southern division of the Egyptian Trail Association was to have other
route issues that needed to be resolved, but fortunately, these were handled
in a more amicable manner. One involved the routing of the trail between
the Washington County towns of Richview and Ashley. Simply stated, the
question was whether to take the "west" road or "east" road into Ashley from
the north out of Richview. Originally, the west road was selected, but when
local vice presidents of the trail traversed this road, they found it to be almost
impassable. The east road, however, was in "first class condition," and a
farmer by the name of Temple who lived along the road had pledged to
drag it and make it an "A No. 1" road. He even consented to "cutting down"
what was known as Logan Hill, the highest hill on the route from Centralia
to DuQuoin, an obstacle to many an autoist at the time. Conversely, south
of Ashley, it was decided the "west road" out of town was the better to take
as there were too many hills on the east road leading into the villages of
Radom and DuBois, which would be an impediment to smooth travel. This

Bird's-eye view of Makanda. *Jackson County Historical Society.*

decision, made in a "cooperative spirit" between the local vice presidents, bypassed the centers of Radom and DuBois, eliminating these villages from the Egyptian Trail route.[75]

A similar decision was made by Dr. Lumpkin that affected the village of Makanda in Jackson County. Rather than the Egyptian Trail Route passing through the center of this small community, as the townspeople wanted, Dr. Lumpkin found a western road on the edge of town to be preferable. Diplomatically, in making his decision, "he admitted the scenery around Makanda, took inspiration from the blue mist that hung over the purple hills, was delighted with the rushing, sparkling waters of Drury Creek, found the people to be courteous and intelligent, but his better judgement decided that the highway passing through the village was not intended as the most practical route for the Egyptian Trail."[76]

A final routing decision in the southern division was made by the people of Boskydell, a small hamlet just north of Makanda. This decision also resolved the question of whether the "east" road or the "west" road into the community would be best. In a classic example of democracy, the question was settled in a town hall–style meeting in the Boskydell Baptist Church. Emanuel Lipe spoke on behalf of the "east" proponents, and James England did the same for the "west" side group. Contemporary accounts indicate that "every farmer, housewife, and daughter have talked nothing but the road subject for the last few days. Nearly three hundred people gathered in Boskydell to vote." The east proposition received 84 votes, the west route 79. A total of 163 votes were cast, and it was said this was the biggest election ever held in Boskydell. As further proof of the residents' commitment to good roads, $188.50 was donated that night to help put the east road in better condition.[77]

The people of Boskydell were not the only ones in the southern division to enthusiastically support the improvement of the Egyptian Trail with contributions of money and labor. In August 1915, it was reported that from Carbondale south to Cobden, the route of the Egyptian Trail had been laid out in one-mile sections that were placed under a "competent supervisor" to oversee the work of grading, dragging and maintaining the road. The adjacent landowners were complimented for not only working with their "muscles and brains" but also for "digging in their pockets" to finance the improvements. It was said, "When the dynamiter and big steam grader and the steel drag have finished their work, the rough places will be made smooth, and the crooked places made straight."[78]

Farmers from this area also met with the Carbondale Chamber of Commerce the following September and made a plea for the businessmen to help raise funds to help "cut-down" some steep hills and build two new bridges along the route. They promised to donate the labor if the funds were raised. They indicated they had already donated about $1,500 worth of work on the road and were reaching the "end of their reserves." Thanks to the prospect of essentially free labor and Carbondale good roads boosters' desire to have the best road along the trail, the funds were raised, and the work was done.[79]

Farther south near Pulaski, the public was invited by local trail vice presidents to participate in work on the route for Good Roads Day, declared to take place in the state on October 20, 1915, by Illinois governor Edward Dunne. The goal for the day was to work on improving the "new road which has been acquired through the Anderson farm on the west side of the Illinois Central right of way three miles north of Pulaski." Participants were encouraged to bring a basket lunch, and if those who were not able to perform manual labor with "pick and shovel" brought along a laborer, they could have the "privilege of bossing for the day." The day was a success, with much work accomplished, and money was also collected from individuals who could not participate in the actual work. These funds were put to use for further trail improvements.

By the end of 1915, the Egyptian Trail through the southern division was completely marked from Centralia to Cairo, and much of the route had been dragged and graded and "put in good shape."

In the summer of 1915, a Captain T.L. Bailey wrote a wonderful essay on the Egyptian Trail in southern Illinois that appeared in many local newspapers, extolling the roadway's virtues and serving as a means to garner support from area residents. An ode of sorts, it is worthy of reprint here.

The Egyptian Trail
By Capt. T.L. Bailey

Following the I.C.R.R. from Chicago to Cairo one passes through the most populous, richest and most variegated section of the great state of Illinois; the wheat belt, the corn belt with its deep black soil that the ages cannot exhaust, and lastly and by no means the least, the great fruit belt of southern Illinois.

One cannot travel from Chicago to Cairo without crossing the spur of the Ozark Mountains that crosses the peninsula of southern Illinois from west to east—from the Mississippi River to the Ohio River. The engineers employed by the I.C.R.R. were wise in their day. They were not only broad, general businessmen but were first class engineers.

The Ashleys and Bucks were the men who located the course of the I.C.R.R. through the hill country of southern Illinois, and they wisely chose the locality that nature had been evolving for untold centuries as if anticipating the advent of the I.C.R.R. and the Egyptian Trail.

Beginning at Boskydell they followed the course of Drury Creek that has its source near Cobden. That bustling little city was in the olden times called South Pass, meaning the south pass through the hill country. The promoters of the Egyptian Trail did the best thing possible when they chose that route.

The Egyptian Trail will be deflected slight at Makanda, the gem city that nestles among the hills and by the grade ascends to the apex of the purple hills. On these hill tops are many beautiful farms and luxurious homes, many farms widening into broad expanses of table lands.

As you look over the hill and dale, a gorgeous panoramic view enchants and delights the vision with its kaleidoscopic grandeur and magnificence rivalling the Valleys of the Hudson or blue Juniata. It is doubtful if in true grandeur and magnificence it is surpassed by the far-famed Rhine or Rhone so long told in story and song. Nothing can be more grand or picturesque than the purple hills of Egypt.

Eight miles to the north is plainly seen Carbondale, with its educational institutions and churches, deservedly called "The Athens of Egypt." Bald

Knob, the highest point of land in Illinois, is in plain view towering high above its companions, while in the distance can be seen the full outline of the hills of Kentucky and Missouri. In plain view from the Trail can be seen great rocks, torn and rent asunder by some terrific convulsion of nature, impressing the mute and astonished beholder with the strength and majesty of the Ruler of the Universe who holds the destiny of the Universe in His Hands.

To the eyes of one who has lived in the atmosphere of the smoky city or become weary of the monotony of flat prairies this change of scenery will well repay a journey of man, many miles.

Passing through Cobden, Anna, Balcom, Dongola, and the "Garden of Egypt" you find that crooked places have been made straight and rough places have been made smooth. Here too, in "Egypt" is found the most congenial climate, a happy blending of temperate and tropical. Is it not a safe prediction to make that when the Egyptian Trail is completed it will be beautiful and embellished and made to bloom like a rose, and for all time continue to be a thing of beauty and joy forever?[80]

TOWNS OF THE SOUTHERN DIVISION OF THE EGYPTIAN TRAIL

Centralia
Marion County, Population 12,491 (1920)

Centralia was established in 1853 by the Illinois Central Railroad and was named for the railroad at the suggestion of John W. Merritt, publisher of the *Salem Advocate* newspaper. Agriculture, the railroad, coal and oil fueled the growth of the community.

Post office established: 1854.

Vice president: J.S. Adams, secretary, Centralia Commercial Club.

Route: From city hall, south on Locust Street to Calumet Street, west to Marion Avenue, south to Thirteenth Street, west to Wabash Avenue, then south through town.

Illinois Central Railroad repair facilities in Centralia. *Author's collection.*

Irvington
Washington County, Population 258 (1920)

Irvington was named for Washington Irving, an American short-story writer, essayist, biographer, historian and diplomat of the early nineteenth century. He is best known for his short stories "Rip Van Winkle" (1819) and "The Legend of Sleepy Hollow" (1820). Alternately, other sources say the name was chosen to honor the father of the first Illinois Central station agent.

Post office established: May 23, 1862.

Vice president: Alva Johnson, bank cashier.

Route: Unknown.

Richview
Washington County, Population 330 (1920)

Richview was laid out in 1839 by W.B. Lindsay and was originally called Richmond. In 1852, the name was changed to Richview because of the elevated site of the old town (one and a half miles from the Illinois Central rail station), which afforded a fine view of the surrounding region.

Post office established: March 1848.

Vice president: Charles P. Cooper, merchant.

Route: Unknown.

Ashley
Washington County, Population 751 (1920)

Ashley was named after Colonel L.W. Ashley, a division engineer for the Illinois Central Railroad, during construction of the railroad in the early 1850s. Prior to this, it was known as Woodrome Settlement.

Post office established: June 1854.

Vice president: Dr. Harry A. Walker, dentist.

Route: Unknown.

Tamora
Perry County, Population 1,115 (1920)

Tamora was named after the Tamaroa, an Illiniwek people. It was given the name by Nelson Holt, an Illinois Central Railroad agent there in 1855. The Tamora Indians were one of the five tribes composing the Illinois Confederacy; the other members of the confederacy were the Michigameas, Kaskaskias, Peorias and Kohakias.

Post office established: March 1855.

Vice president: Howard Haines, bank cashier

Route: Walnut Street through town.

DuQuoin
Perry County, Population 7,285 (1920)

DuQuoin was named after an Illiniwek Native American, Chief Jean Baptiste Ducoigne of the Kaskaskia. He was killed by the Shawnee tribes in 1802. The town was founded in 1844 in the area where Old Du Quoin now stands. Later, in 1853, when the Illinois Central Railroad lines were completed, the residents and new settlers moved westward and laid out the present-day city of Du Quoin near the railroad station.

Brick pavement on Washington Street, a part of the Egyptian Trail, in DuQuoin. *IDOT.*

Post office established: March 1844.

Vice president: James Forester, coal mine owner

Route: Main Street east to Washington Street, south on Washington Street through town.

Elkville
Jackson County, Population 990 (1920)

Elkville was named for the elk that in the early days of the settlement came from the adjacent prairies to frequent the salt licks near the original town site. Along the Illinois Central Railroad, it was founded in 1857 and incorporated as a village in 1893.

Vice president: William S. Boone, druggist.

Route: Unknown.

View of business section in Elkville. *Jackson County Historical Society.*

View of business section in Desoto. *Jackson County Historical Society.*

DeSoto
Jackson County, Population 703 (1920)

DeSoto was named in honor of Fernando de Soto, the famous Spanish explorer. The town site was laid out in 1854, with the arrival of the Illinois Central Railroad, and a post office was established in 1855.

Vice president: Henry Zacher, miller.

Route: Chestnut Street through town.

Carbondale
Jackson County, Population 6,207 (1920)

Carbondale was named by Daniel Bush, one of its founders, for the large deposits of coal found in the area. The Illinois Central Railroad's first train through Carbondale went through town on Independence Day 1854. Southern Illinois Normal University was founded in the city in 1874. As an educational and cultural center in southern Illinois, it is known as the "Athens of Egypt."

Post office established: February 27, 1854.

Incorporated as a city: 1869.

Vice president: Henry Fraley, grocer.

Route: South on Illinois Avenue.

Illinois Avenue, the route of the Egyptian Trail through Carbondale. *Author's collection.*

Boskydell
Jackson County, Unincorporated

Boskydell translates to "brush valley"; the town was named by the Reverend J.L. Hawkins of Carbondale. As early as 1852, Illinois Central Railroad surveyors discovered good deposits of sandstone in the area. These were quarried and used to build the railroad's bridges and abutments. The sandstone, with its warm, reddish-brown color, was also used in construction of some local notable buildings, including the Illinois state capitol.

Post office established: July 24, 1885.[81]

Vice president: Emanuel Lipe, farmer.

Route: Unknown.

Cobden
Union County, Population 944 (1920)

Cobden was named in 1859 after Sir Richard Cobden, an English statesman and member of Parliament, who was a large shareholder of the Illinois Central Railroad and who traveled the line in 1858. The town was formerly called South Pass and is the center of vegetable- and fruit-growing country.

Post office established: February 8, 1858, as South Pass; name changed to Cobden on June 5, 1873.

Vice president: S. Roy Green, merchant.

Route: Oak Street east to Front Street, Front Street south through town.

Fruit and vegetable basket manufacturing in Cobden. *Library of Congress.*

Anna
Union County, Population 3,019 (1920)

Anna was platted on March 3, 1854, after the Illinois Central Railroad established a station there. It was founded by Winstead Davie and named after Anna Willard Davie, his wife. The post office was established on March 14, 1855, and the town was incorporated on February 16, 1865.

Anna boasts some of the largest strawberry farms in the U.S. It is also the home of a state hospital for the insane, comprising magnificent buildings and beautiful grounds. The Union Academy of Southern Illinois is but one of its fine educational institutions. A drive around the loop—31 miles of thoroughly enjoyable driving over good roads—starts at Anna, passes by the lakes west of Anna, thru Jonesboro, one of the oldest towns in the state, thru rich Mississippi River farmlands and alfalfa fields, and along the riverfront for eight miles showing a panorama of scenic splendor.[82]

Vice president: Emmett S. Alden, merchant.
Route: Vienna Street east through town.

A business district view of Anna. *IDOT.*

Dongola
Union County, Population 660 (1920)

Dongola was laid out in 1857 as a stop along the Illinois Central Railroad by Ebeni Leavenworth, an engineer for the railroad. A post office known as Unionville had been established on November 9, 1855, but the name was changed to Dongola, on April 16, 1857, after Dongola, Sudan.

Vice president: Henry J. Neibauer, bank president.

Route: Front Street through town.

Wetaug
Pulaski County, Unincorporated

Wetaug was named by George Watson, a division superintendent of the Illinois Central, who formerly lived in a small town by the same name in Massachusetts. In the Ojibway Indian dialect, the word means "gambler."

Post office established: December 6, 1856.

Vice president: None.

Route: Unknown.

Ullin
Pulaski County, Population 652 (1920)

Ullin, located along the Illinois Central in the early 1850s, was reportedly named after Ullin, Fingal's bard in the poems of Ossian, published by the Scottish poet James Macpherson in the 1760s. Other sources suggest it was named for its first postmaster, Samuel Ulen. A post office opened on January 5, 1856, and the village was platted the following year. Ullin incorporated in 1900.

Vice president: Dr. John B. Mathis, physician.

Route: Locust Street south through town.

Pulaski
Pulaski County, Population 518 (1920)

Pulaski was named in honor of Count Casmir Pulaski, a Polish soldier who fought in the Revolutionary War and became a brigadier general in the American army. It was founded in 1852 as a construction camp along the Illinois Central Railroad. A post office was established on May 27, 1856. The village was initially known as Camp Pulaski, but the "Camp" was dropped from the name in 1872. Pulaski incorporated in 1898.

Vice president: Dr. John B. Mathis, physician.

Route: Unknown.

Villa Ridge
Pulaski County, unincorporated

Villa Ridge was established along the Illinois Central in 1852. A post office was established on August 12, 1853, and named Valley Forge; the name was changed to Villa Ridge on June 26, 1861. Villa Ridge was named by a daughter of the local doctor, Doctor Arter, after the farm the family settled on in 1837.

Vice president: None

Route: Unknown.

Mounds
Pulaski County, Population 2,661 (1920)

Mounds derives its name from the Indian mounds in the vicinity of the town. It was founded about 1886 as a company town for the Illinois Central Railroad. The post office was established as early as 1865 as Junction, and its name changed to Mounds Junction in 1886, to Beechwood in 1892 and, finally, to Mounds on October 15, 1903.

Car in ravine in Jackson County. *Jackson County Historical Museum.*

Incorporated: February 1904.

Vice president: B. King.

Route: The "government" road to First Street, west to the Illinois Central Railroad depot, then north on Front Street through town.

Cairo
Alexander County, Population 15,203 (1920)

In 1818, John Comegys, Shadrack Bond and others contracted on 1,800 acres of land near the mouth of the Ohio River and obtained a charter from the territorial legislature under the name City and Bank of Cairo.

By its geographical location, nature intended Cairo to be a hub around which should center the business activities of a great portion of the Mississippi valley. Thirty million people are within twelve hours ride of this city. Located at the junction of the Mississippi and Ohio rivers, in the extreme southern part of Illinois, it is served by five of the great railroad trunks and occupies an advantageous commercial position. Its principal industries are lumber and wood working, grain and grain products, and the manufacture of pearl buttons, silos, and ready cut houses. It has splendid schools, churches, hotels, parks, modern and up-to-date retail establishments, theatres, good society, and a healthful climate. Cairo offers the advantages of an up-to-date community possessing all the attributes which combine to make an ideal location.

The Good Roads Committee of the association of Commerce, with the cooperation of the Cairo Automobile Club, is very active in the promotion of better roads, resulting in twenty miles of brick paved streets in the city and fifty miles of rock and gravel macadam in Alexander and Pulaski County. Ferries are regularly operated from Cairo across both the Ohio and Mississippi rivers, giving good service to tourists into the states of Missouri and Kentucky.[83]

Post office established: November 8, 1837, as Mouth of Ohio; name changed to Cairo on September 16, 1839.

Vice president: W.F. Crossley, Interurban vice president.

Route: From the Ohio River west on Sixth Street to Washington Avenue, north on Washington Avenue, then north on Sycamore Street through town following the Mound City Road.

Downtown street and arch view in Cairo. *Author's collection.*

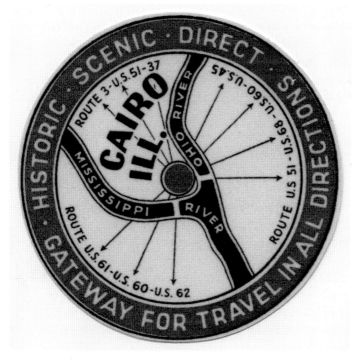

Advertisement touting Cairo and the roads leading to it. *Author's collection.*

THE ROAD DRAG

Perhaps nothing helped to improve the over two million miles of rural dirt roads in the United States at the start of the twentieth century more than the "split log" road drag invented by David Ward King.

Born and educated in Springfield, Ohio, David Ward King (1857–1920), who was known as D. Ward King, moved to rural Maitland, Missouri, after his marriage in 1881 and began life as a farmer. In 1896, he demonstrated the use of his simple invention, dubbed the King Road Drag or the split-log drag, which consisted of two split logs attached by crossbeams and hitched with a loop of chain to horses, to be dragged along a stretch of rutted, muddy road until it was smooth. His rudimentary road grader had the effect not only of flattening and compacting muddy soil but also of creating a crest in the center of the road, sloping down at each side, so that the rain would run off the packed surface into the ditch. This basic scheme had a revolutionary effect on rural life. Farmers were often mired in mud on the roads to their fields or into town, their most powerful draft horses unable to contend with wagon wheels sunken into deep ruts after heavy rains. Use of King's drag soon made their roads not only passable but also faster and safer to travel, which saved time and money for all in the community.

In 1903, King was employed by the Chicago and Northwestern Transportation Co. to promote his product across the country as part of their "Good Roads Campaign," giving lectures and demonstrations. King patented the King Road Drag (U.S. Patent 884,497 and U.S. Patent 1,102,671) in 1908 and later improved it in 1914. The United States Patent Office called his invention a "Road Grader," but King referred to it as a "split log drag" or the "King Road Drag."

Although King patented his invention, the simple design made it difficult to enforce patent rights, so farmers were encouraged to build and make use of their own versions of the road drag. King made a decent living for years on the lecture circuit, presenting in forty-six of the forty-eight existing states and Canada. His midwestern education made him an eloquent, dynamic speaker, and his talks were often sold out. The invention of the

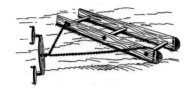

How To Make Good Dirt Roads

The Split Log Drag

Easy to make—easy to run—and which, rightly used, convinces the unconvinced, converts the unconverted, makes rough roads smooth, and soft roads hard. A simple implement made on the farm, which will transform the roads of the corn and grass belt.

"The Great Highway," promotional road drag brochure of D. Ward King. *National Museum of American History.*

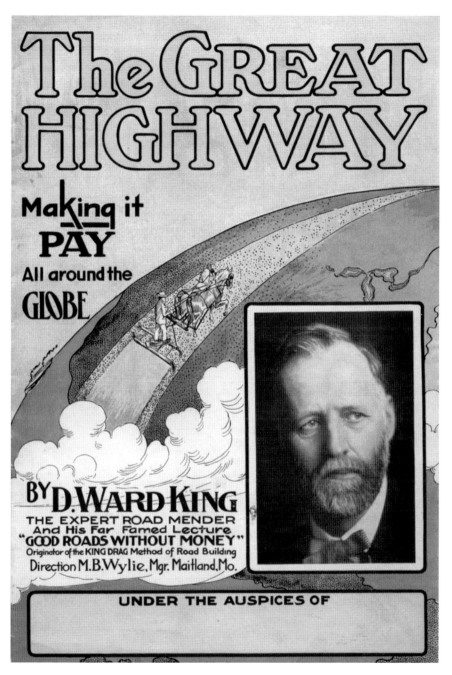

Instructions on how to build a road drag. *National Museum of American History.*

road drag and its almost evangelical use across the country has been credited for increased automobile use in the early part of the century, as well as the advent of parcel post delivery and mail-order catalogs supply to rural areas.

So influential was King's split log drag that it inspired a poem for the Western Mutual Life Insurance Company of Council Bluffs, Iowa. Written by Eulalie Andreas of Davenport, Iowa, the poem was intended to stimulate interest in his drag and make companies realize that good roads help business everywhere.

> *Oh! Here's to the Man with the Drag and a team!*
> *And here's to the genius who tho't of the scheme!*
> *To the man with the DRAG all honor is due*
> *And glory to him who invented it too.*
> *"Good roads" he pleads, "Good roads" is his cry.*
> *"Good roads" jeers the farmer, "in the sweet bye and bye."*
> *But while they are sitting and sighing "alas,"*
> *And waiting a road-bill, legislature to pass,*
> *A man up and doing has thought of a way*
> *To fill in the ruts and to level the clay;*
> *But waiting for any slow process law*
> *He gives us a method direct as a saw.*
> *He says, "get me some planks Sir, and hitch to your team*
> *And drive right ahead! Why, you'll think it's a dream*
> *The way these old roads will straighten out flat—*
> *And wonder why man n'er before tho't of that."*
> *He asks for no patent, no money wants he,*
> *For good of mankind he is giving it free.*
> *Just try it (if prone to discredit the plan)—*
> *You'll find it a wonderful blessing to man.*
> *But, meanwhile the laggards they laugh in distrust*
> *And sitting on barrels the things is discussed.*
> *"By gosh," they protest, "Why, this fool of a man*
> *He thinks he can josh us—but not much he can!*
> *Why who ever heard of a pavin' with planks*
> *A-swingin' from hosses! Guess not, Sir—no thanks!"*
> *But the live one today is trying the Drag*
> *And soon of his roadway he justly can brag.*
> *To the man with Drag all honor is due!*
> *And glory to him who invented it too!*
> *So here's to the man who discovered the way!*
> *And here's to the farmer who works it, TODAY!*[84]

Chapter 6

THE EGYPTIAN TRAIL AND THE $60 MILLION ROAD BOND ISSUE

A s 1916 rolled around, President Lumpkin, Secretary-Treasurer Tucker, the division officers and all the Egyptian Trail vice presidents could look back on the last six months with a bit of pride. In that short period of time, the Egyptian Trail had gone from an idea to a fully routed, marked and largely improved earthen roadway stretching from Cairo to Chicago. The Egyptian Trail had figuratively and literally been put "on the map" of the state of Illinois.

In early 1916, trail vice presidents were preparing for spring dragging, grading and other annual improvements necessary as a result of winter snows and spring rains that would routinely damage road surfaces. The Egyptian Trail Association held its annual meeting in October that year in Mattoon. In addition to trail vice presidents discussing activities during the past year, many also happily reported a marked increase in traffic coming through their towns. A citizen of Thomasboro in Champaign County told of counting two hundred automobiles passing through town in a forty-five-minute period.[85] President Lumpkin also made sure a major topic of discussion at the meeting was lobbying. It was now time for local vice presidents to initiate lobbying efforts to secure government funding to better improve the trail, with the goal of making it a fully "hard surfaced" highway.

President Lumpkin and association members also discussed the shortfall and delay in road improvements that still existed even after passage of the Tice Law in 1913. Despite the fact that government aid was now being distributed directly to only the 102 counties of the

By the mid-teens, road conditions could still be a muddy "mess." *The University of Michigan— the Lincoln Highway Collection.*

Farmer and horse team pulling a car out of the mud. *The University of Michigan—the Lincoln Highway Collection.*

state—far less cumbersome than to the 1,432 townships in the state, as it was before the law was enacted—this still resulted in a system where counties were only concerned about their own road problems, resulting in a patchwork of improvements that frequently had no connection outside their jurisdictions. Furthermore, the lack of a systematic method of managing road improvements in specific geographical areas increased costs, as there were no efficiencies gained by coordinating contracts and contractors when smaller paving jobs were spread all across the state. Administrative and construction costs increased, which meant less paving work could be done.

Several local Egyptian Trail vice presidents were also on the board of directors of the Illinois Highway Improvement Association. These included their president, William G. Edens of Chicago, second vice president Charles Kiler of Champaign and third vice president C.G. Miller of Cairo. These men and the Illinois Highway Improvement Association were ardent good roads proponents and continued to study the highway funding issue. At the annual meeting, they told of a potential proposal for a substantial bond issue to provide funds for state-supervised construction of a statewide system of highways. Egyptian Trail leaders were supportive of this and encouraged them to pursue the change.

The issue was discussed more fully at the fifth annual convention of the Illinois Highway Improvement Association in Danville on December 19, 1916. There was no doubt that a change in how state road funding was administered was needed, and the main question at the convention centered on the actual amount of bonds to issue. At first it was thought $40 million would be sufficient; that number then increased to $50 million. At the meeting, delegates heard a presentation from Illinois State Highway superintendent Samuel Bradt, who proposed a $60 million bond issue to finance the improvement of 4,000 miles (this number later increased to 4,800) of state highways in Illinois.[86]

Improvement Association delegates agreed, passed a resolution to that effect and called for their leaders to secure support of the bonding proposal from the governor, Illinois state representatives and senators.

Frank O. Lowden, a farmer, had just been elected governor in November but had a wide grasp of the good roads issue. He was supportive of the bonding proposal, with one exception. The proposal called for the bond interest payments to be split between the motor license fee fund and the general fund of the state. He was in favor of the full interest payments being paid for by motor license fees. This was agreed to.[87]

Legislators were lined up to present bills in their respective houses and lobby their colleagues. The bills passed in the Illinois house on April 12, 1917, and in the senate a week later. Since the bond issue required the approval of Illinois voters, now it was just a matter of time before the referendum question was decided at the election to take place on November 5, 1918, fully eighteen months away.[88]

Even though the election was a year and a half away, no time was wasted preparing for it and educating the voters on the importance of this proposition to all residents of the state. To help with this, the state highway department prepared details on the routes of the forty-six State Bond Improved roadways that were to be a part of this program. Portions of the Egyptian Trail were part of three of them. The Egyptian Trail was to be fully improved for its length from Cairo through Kankakee, with the exception of a small segment from Watson to Alma, south of Effingham. From Kankakee to Chicago, the Dixie Highway route was selected through Momence and then northward to be the State Bond Improved road.

Above: Governor Frank Loden. *Library of Congress.*

Opposite: Sample bond issue promotional flyer. *Illinois Highway Improvement Association.*

The Egyptian trail was included in:

STATE BOND IMPROVED ROUTE 2: Beginning in a public highway near Beloit, Wisconsin, and running along such a highway in a generally southerly direction to Cairo, affording Rockford, Oregon, Dixon, Mendota, Peru, LaSalle, El Paso, Bloomington, Clinton, Decatur, Pana, Vandalia, Centralia, Du Quoin, Carbondale, Anna, Cairo and the intervening communities reasonable connections with each other. (The section from Centralia to Cairo was the Egyptian Trail.)

STATE BOND IMPROVED ROUTE 12: Beginning in a public highway at the Indiana state line east of Lawrenceville and running along such a highway in a westerly direction to East St. Louis, affording Lawrenceville, Olney, Flora, Salem, Carly, Lebanon, East St. Louis and the intervening communities reasonable connections with each other. (The section from Salem to Sandoval was the Egyptian Trail.)

WORKINGMEN!

BE SURE TO PUT AN **"X"** OPPOSITE

"YES"

FOR

GOOD ROADS BONDS

THE LAST PROPOSITION ON THE LITTLE BALLOT IN CHICAGO

$30,000,000 of the $60,000,000 Will Go to Labor

SPECIAL WARNING—If you vote at the Election next Tuesday and fail to vote for the Good Roads Bonds, *your vote will be counted against the proposition* and labor will be among the chief losers.

What Chicago's Street Car Men's Union Says:

Whereas, the funds to pay both the principal and interest on the bonds are to be secured from State motor vehicle license fees, the bonds to be marketed and the work to commence after the close of the war, giving a return to labor of more than $30,000,000 in construction work, while the total cost will be borne by those who own automobiles, the funds coming from the motor license fees solely—

Resolved, That Division 241 of the Amalgamated Association of Street and Electric Railway Employes of America indorse this proposition and urge upon our members the necessity of voting for it at the November election, a majority of all votes cast at this election being required for its adoption.

What the Chicago Federation of Labor Says:

"*Resolved,* That we give hearty indorsement to the proposed $60,000,000 bond issue."

INDORSED ALSO BY

Chicago Federation of Musicians
Illinois State Federation of Miners
Typographical Union No. 16
Quincy Trades and Labor Assembly
Springfield Federation of Labor
Division No. 1, Order of Railway Conductors
Brotherhood of Threshermen
W. M. Hobbs Lodge No. 4, P. H. Morrissey Lodge No. 62, At Last Lodge No. 456 and Columbian Lodge No. 479 Brotherhood of Railroad Trainmen

Jack Christie Division No. 231 and John Player Divisions No. 458 and No. 645, Brotherhood of Locomotive Engineers
Lodge No. 217, Brotherhood of Locomotive Firemen and Enginemen
Bricklayers and Stone Masons' Union of Chicago
Central Trades and Labor Assembly of Bloomington
Garden City Branch No. 11, Chicago Letter Carriers' Association

NO TAX AGAINST REAL ESTATE

NO BURDEN ON YOUR HOME

All the Cost Placed Upon Automobile Owners

THIS IS A WISE MEASURE FOR THE WORKINGMAN TO SUPPORT

This Advertisement Paid For by the Associated Roads Organizations of Chicago and Cook County

STATE BOND IMPROVED ROUTE 25: Beginning in a public highway at Kankakee and running along such a highway in a general southerly direction to Fairfield, affording Kankakee, Gilman, Paxton, Champaign, Tuscola, Mattoon, Effingham, Toliver, Louisville, Flora, Fairfield and the intervening communities reasonable connections with each other. (The section from Kankakee to Effingham was the Egyptian Trail.)[89]

Members of the Illinois Highway Improvement Association and Edens participated vigorously in the campaign to ensure passage of this referendum. At their convention in Bloomington held on October 24, 1917, they agreed to take up the charge given them by Governor Lowden to "carry the campaign into every county and township" in the state.

"Carry the campaign" they did. They produced over six million educational maps, folders, posters, booklets and pamphlets that were distributed throughout the state. They coordinated in their efforts with various business, agricultural and labor organizations to ensure the message was constantly being put in front of the voters in various constituencies. They elicited newspapers to support the effort by printing prepared materials sent to them in the months before the election. A movie titled *Thru Illinois: Over Unchanged Roads in a World of Change* was even produced by the association and shown in theaters to highlight the state of Illinois roads to those who may not have traveled far enough from home to experience them.[90]

All these efforts paid off, and the referendum on the bond issue passed overwhelmingly—661,815 to 154,396. The measure also carried in every county of the state.[91]

The campaign was a success, but it was to hit an anticipated snag in implementation from the outset. At the time of the referendum, the United States was a nation at war, although the war, providentially, would end within two weeks of the vote. The governor and good roads advocates recognized that the war posed labor and material shortage challenges and took this into account in their campaigning for the passage of the bond issue. The governor pledged that bonds would not be marketed until sufficient time had passed and the labor and material shortage situation had settled after the war. They understood that doing so beforehand would likely result in prohibitive prices, which would dramatically reduce the purchasing power of the bonds.[92]

Though the first bonds were not marketed until the end of 1921,[93] work started in 1919, and before the close of the year, 254.78 miles of hard roads

Sample bond issue promotional flyers. *Illinois Highway Improvement Association.*

were constructed under the bond issue. In 1920, that number increased to 365.52 miles, which fell far short of the 1,000-mile goal that state highway superintendent Bradt had set for the year. In a meeting with Douglas County highway representatives in Champaign County in January 1920, Bradt indicated that the state had placed orders for 3,000,000 barrels of cement but was only being promised 125,000 barrels for the year. Labor was not an issue, but materials certainly were.[94] The situation began to ease, and by 1922 and 1923, paving of bond-issue roads had reached anticipated levels, with 1,085.02 miles and 1,229.48 miles paved in those years, respectively.[95]

Another issue that was to delay paving of the Egyptian Trail, particularly in parts of the northern and central divisions, was the time needed to survey, negotiate for and acquire rights of way from landowners along the Illinois Central Railroad to allow the new paved road to parallel the railroad as closely as possible. As an example, in Iroquois County, the town of Chebanse is ten miles east of Loda at the south end of the county. Since the original routing of the Egyptian Trail followed township or sectional roads in these areas, the route had to zigzag or stairstep constantly in order to preserve its general alignment with the railroad. This added mileage to the route and also necessitated crossing the rail tracks several times, creating a safety hazard. The only places where the roadway followed the railroad diagonally was either in town centers or about seven miles between Clifton and Ashkum and about nine miles between Buckley and the south county line.[96] The State Bond Road Improvements were to rectify this situation basically in sections as needed from Kankakee south to Salem.

President Lumpkin and Egyptian Trail leaders were becoming anxious about the progress of paving in 1920 but understood that material shortages were not under the control of the state highway department and did not press the issue at the time. Lumpkin was also concerned about the state highway commission potentially making changes to State Bond Improvement routes to be paved that would deviate from some original Egyptian Trail communities. This was particularly true in Champaign County and between the Douglas and Coles County towns of Arcola and Mattoon on what was the State Bond Issue Route 25 portion of the trail.

To forestall any of these issues, Lumpkin arranged for a meeting with Samuel Bradt, superintendent of the highway department, along with his assistant and chief highway engineer, that was held at the Champaign County courthouse in Urbana on April 16, 1920. News accounts indicate that people came from as far as Effingham and Kankakee to attend and that close to five hundred "enthusiastic" supporters filled the courtroom to standing room only.

Bradt led the meeting and allowed representatives, mostly trail vice presidents, from various communities to speak. Almost to a man, they were in favor of keeping the route through the original trail communities. Secretary-Treasurer Tucker "emphasized the necessity for keeping faith with the people who had worked and toiled to make possible the bond issue, believing when they voted for 'Route 25' that they were voting for the Egyptian Trail." Tucker asked permission to have those at the meeting who endorsed the Egyptian Trail stand up, and "the crowd stood up and cheered in such numbers that it looked as if the crowd was 100 percent loyal to the Egyptian Trail."

The highway men apparently got the message, as Bradt concluded the meeting with the statement that an early decision would be made regarding any changes, but "he believed it would please 99-percent of the people along

Attention Egyptian Trail Boosters

To All Vice-Presidents, Friends, and Those Living Adjacent to the Egyptian Trail, From Chicago to Cairo:

Like you, the general officers of this trail have labored hard to help pull Illinois out of the mud, from the time this trail was organized in 1915, up to the present time. We all know the way we have worked and helped and hoped and prayed to the end that this trail might some day be a hard surfaced road. And this is what we want to talk to you about.

The success of the $60,000,000 Bond Election was due largely to trail organizations and motorists, both of whom worked like Trojans to carry the election and are now carrying the financial burden of the roads we haven't got, NEVER WILL GET, during our life time. The department say they have built 154 miles of road this year. Most of this is on the government aid roads, for a portion of which the government pays. Take 4,800 miles as the $60,000,000 bond system and figure for yourself how long it will take the administration's highway department to complete it all at the rate of 154 miles per year, provided after the politicians have secured the roads they want there is any money left with which to build the rest. It will be 31 years at the present rate. And this is a fair average and they got a good start last year.

It is not likely that the highway administration will be changed if the administration candidate, John Oglesby, is elected governor. They are making their campaign on the administration's record and that means that the administration's policies will either be endorsed or rejected at the polls, Wednesday, September 15.

Len Small, also a Republican candidate for the nomination for governor, is on record as having promised the people some speed in road building. He says, "I favor and shall vigorously push to completion the development of Illinois' hard road system, which has been emphatically approved by the people." It is the opinion of the general officers of The Egyptian Trail, who are sending out this appeal and paying for it out of their own pockets that the Egyptian Trail will never be built so long as there remains unbuilt any part of the proposed highway system that the present administration's political friends are interested in

In plain words we will never get any road under the Lowden administration of affairs, and our

only hope therefore is to nominate Len Small and elect him governor of Illinois so we will get some.

We believe the Egyptian Trail from Chicago to Cairo is the biggest and most important road proposition in the State of Illinois We believe the rapid completion of the hard roads program in Illinois is of more vital interest to every Illinoisian than who is Governor of Illinois, whether John Oglesby, Len Small, or J. Hamilton Lewis. We put the road system first, then ally ourselves with the man who says he will build them, and backs his promise with performance. That man is Len Small. We believe he will "deliver the goods" on hard roads in Illinois. The Lowden administration has tried and failed. We have everything to gain and nothing to lose by a change.

We did not want to get the Egyptian Trail in politics and we would not, were it not for the fact that the highway department has not kept faith with us in its promises, in its detailing of routes, or with its bounden duty to build hard roads as fast as they can and without regard to political fear or favor. If we must get into politics in order to get something done, let's start right now. We were forced to take this stand and we propose to maintain it until we succeed.

If you think the State Public Utilities Commission needs a shake up or abolishment, what do you think ought to be done with the State Highway Department?

We urge every man and woman voter, who lives adjacent to the Egyptian Trail, to work unceasingly from now until primary day to help nominate Len Small for governor, the man who promises to complete the hard road system. And this we do in all earnestness and sincerity, with one purpose in view, the hard surfacing of the Egyptian Trail and the placing of its detail on main, broad, well-traveled highways without regard as to whether Senator Dunlay or any other politician lives along it, or has property on it.

Vote for this change and get all your friends to do so

THE EGPTIAN TRAIL ASSOCIATION,

Dr. I A. Lumpkin, President
E. B. Tucker, Secretary.
General Office: Mattoon, Illinois.

BUILD THE EGYPTIAN TRAIL FIRST--NOT LAST

Lumpkin/Tucker bond issue advertisement. *Newspaperarchives.com.*

the route."[97] However "rosy" and comforting the superintendent's statement at the conclusion of the meeting may have seemed to the audience, it turned out that when the decision was made, the route deviations were indeed selected, thereby eliminating towns like Humboldt and Arcola and other sections of the original Egyptian Trail from the bond issue route to be paved.

Naturally, President Lumpkin and Secretary-Treasurer Tucker felt betrayed by this decision and sought redress. It so happened that 1920 was a gubernatorial election year in Illinois, and while not wanting to embroil the Egyptian Trail Association in politics, they believed the election was the only way they could get the results needed. Lumpkin and Tucker personally paid for long op-ed pieces identified as "political advertisements" in newspapers that circulated along the trail, urging trail supporters to vote for Len Small, a Kankakee Republican candidate for governor, in that party's September 15 primary.

The lengthy ads also detailed Lumpkin and Tucker's grievances with the state highway department, one of which was that the route the department selected between Arcola and Mattoon was a

> *blind lane, sparsely settled, narrow road, that will require dedication of land on either side to make it conform to specifications, and will also require the right of way either by donation, purchase or condemnation through farmland. In other words so anxious were they to defeat us that they ignored a wide, main-traveled and well-kept highway to pick out a blind lane that starts from nowhere and runs to the same place.*

Other grievances centered around the new route selected from Champaign to Savoy and the fact that the original trail towns south of Effingham from Watson to Salem had been eliminated from State Bond Improvement Route 25 at the outset of planning for paving even before the $60 million bond issue was approved. Lumpkin and Tucker's ad in a rebuke to the highway department said,

> *There is a section of the trail, however, between Champaign and Savoy that the Department did detail as part of the road. Senator Dunlap lives on this stretch between Savoy and Champaign, and also owns orchard land on the proposed road between Effingham and Flora. This latter road is the one that was substituted at the eleventh hour for the trail road between Effingham and Salem and Centralia. Do you get the point? The state highway department is taking good care of its political friends but where do you come in?[98]*

Concrete paving work near Champaign. *Champaign County History Museum.*

Lumpkin and Tucker were offended that political cronyism had taken precedent over the common good of all along the route in this decision. In the end, Len Small was elected governor of Illinois in 1920, and the route deviations in Champaign, Douglas and Coles Counties were eventually rescinded and never implemented.

During the early 1920s, the road materials shortage eased and completed paved mileage under the bond issue program had progressed to the levels the state anticipated. The year 1923 was a banner one for paving work on the bond-issue roads that comprised the Egyptian Trail. Newspapers along the route were replete with articles like these regarding the status of paving in their area.

> *Albert Wright, commissioner of highways of Tuscola township, in order that there will be no delay in building the stretch of highway from Arcola to Tuscola, has been busy getting the right of way. He reports that there are only five farmers owning land between Tuscola and Arcola Township and he has seen all of them. The owners are asking from $275 to $300 an acre for a 60-foot strip through their farms.[99]*

> *Clark Brothers of Terre Haute, Ind., the contractors who will build the pavement from Onarga to Paxton on the Egyptian Trail, have erected two large concrete sheds in Buckley. One shed has eleven sections and the other*

Another view of concrete paving work near Champaign. *Champaign County History Museum.*

thirteen. Twenty carloads of cement will be stored in this city and similar buildings will be erected at Del Rey and Onarga.[100]

The grade has been completed and the gang started laying concrete between Kankakee and Chebanse. The contractors said that they expect to lay at least 600 feet per day, and complete the work between Kankakee and Chebanse this summer.[101]

Kankakee, Ill: Shanks and Gannon, working on the Egyptian Trail, west on Jeffrey Street and south to Chebanse, have done four miles, with five more to complete. Their job ends at the county mark at Chebanse.[102]

On August 1, when William "Bill" McNeely's road construction organization broke a world's record by pouring 1,761 lineal feet of eighteen foot concrete slab, The Journal Gazette predicted that "Bill" was shooting for a new high mark of 2,000 feet, and that sooner or later he would obtain it.

The prediction has come true, for on Tuesday, August 14, this highly perfected and well equipped organization did that very thing, and seventeen feet more, the total for the day's work being 2,017 lineal feet....

The people of this vicinity are very fortunate indeed in that the McNeely Company secured this contract on Route 25, as some parts of the state, the contractors are only doing one-fourth and even less than the McNeely Company is doing.[103]

Gilman, Ill.: The McMahon Construction Company is now at the east city limits with the Egyptian Trail from the north and will probably finish up the stretch on Crescent Street this week. The company is pushing the work with the upmost rapidity and are working from dawn until dark. During the past week they have been laying an average of from 700 to 800 feet of road on this section.

The company had another mixing machine, an unloading crane and a number of additional trucks sent to Gilman last week, and this outfit is now being used on the stretch south of Gilman, with two machines in operation that are putting down 1,300 to 1,400 feet of road each day.[104]

The Shelton residence at the south end of Railroad Avenue is being moved to a position forty feet east of its present location to make way for the new hard road right of way route 25, better known as the Egyptian Trail. O'Connor and Sons, contractors, who have completed the hard road from Ludlow to the creek bridge, a distance of two and a half miles, will move their equipment to Paxton so they may start building south from Ottawa Road.[105]

Work like this continued, and in a rare moment of celebration, Governor Small and a delegation of dignitaries helped commemorate the completion of Route 25, the Egyptian Trail, from Effingham to Tuscola on October 23, 1923. Accompanied by a band, Small and his party made stops for brief

Preparation work for laying base for brick pavement near Champaign. *Champaign County History Museum.*

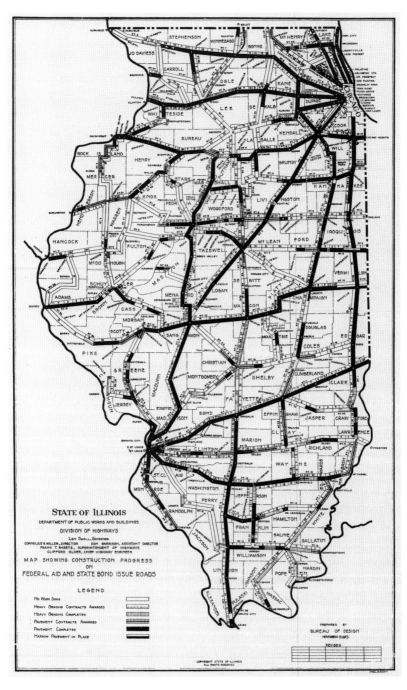

Road map from 1923 showing construction progress on bond issue roadways.
Illinois Secretary of State.

concerts and addresses in Humboldt, Arcola, Tuscola and Mattoon. Plans had been made for Small to attend a large banquet that evening but were abandoned as he had to return to Springfield for state business. This is the only known celebration commemorating completion of paving along the Egyptian Trail.[106]

By 1924, the same year that Illinois surpassed one million registered vehicles, twelve thousand state workers managed to pave 1,230 miles of new roads with Portland concrete at a cost of roughly $30,000 per mile. This essentially completed paving on all the bond issue roadways, including those that composed the Egyptian Trail. At mid-decade, Illinois led all states in the nation with 5,315 miles of concrete paved roads.[107]

After a decade of hard work and perseverance, President Lumpkin and all Egyptian Trail supporters had achieved a remarkable feat—going from a trail filled with rutted dirt roads to one that was *almost* fully concrete paved. There was now only the section between Kankakee and Chicago that still needed to be addressed.

COLONEL WILLIAM G. EDENS

William G. Edens was a well-known champion of and arguably the "Father of the Illinois Good Roads Movement." He was the first president of the Illinois Highway Improvement Association, and it was largely attributable to his tireless efforts and organizational ability that Illinois voted in the $60 million bond issue to improve 4,800 miles of highways in the state in 1918.

Edens built a career in railroads, labor and banking and was active in Republican politics. His life would be regarded along the lines of a traditional American success story. Born in Richmond, Indiana, on November 27, 1863, he was on his own at age fourteen and started working as a telegraph messenger boy. He then became a mail carrier and next took a job as an assistant to a railroad stationmaster. He worked for many years on the railroad, filling a variety of jobs from brakeman to conductor.

Edens was an organizing officer of the Brotherhood of Railroad Trainmen and was vice grand master of the organization. He later became state organizer of the Illinois Republican League and was on the staff of the Republican National Committee. In October 1897, he was appointed by President McKinley to be assistant general superintendent of the free delivery system in the post office department and served until 1904, when he resigned to again become state organizer of the Illinois Republican League during the national election campaign that year.

Edens began his banking career in 1905, when he was employed with the Central Trust Company of Chicago as manager of the new business department. In 1909, he was made assistant secretary of the company and became its vice president in 1919. He retired from banking in 1931.

During World War I, Edens was an honorary recruiting officer for the U.S. War Department and also served in the 17th Engineers Regiment of the American Expeditionary Forces and the 108th Illinois Engineers Division. He was recognized for his recruiting efforts and given the honorary title of colonel, which he proudly used for the rest of his life.

Colonel William G. Edens. *The University of Michigan—the Lincoln Highway Collection.*

As a tribute to his lifelong interest in good roads, the Cook County Board of Commissioners voted to name a new north suburban highway after him. Now known as the Edens Expressway, the highway was dedicated in ceremonies on October 9, 1949, and was finished and "officially" opened on December 20, 1951. Remarkably, Edens never owned or drove a car in his life.

Colonel Edens died on November 15, 1957, and is interred in Memorial Park Cemetery in Skokie, Illinois.[108]

Chapter 7

SUCCESSOR ROUTES AND THE EGYPTIAN TRAIL LEGACY

I n the ten years between the establishment of the Egyptian Trail and the completion of the state bond improvement of roads, the Illinois highway department had gone from a small operation to one that was firmly in control of planning, supervising construction of and the ongoing maintenance of the roadways in Illinois. To reinforce this, Colonel C.R. Miller, director of the department of public works and buildings, the agency in charge of highways, and Frank T. Sheets, chief state highway engineer, issued a statement in January 1925 regarding establishment of new highway or trail organizations. The statement indicated:

> *Many individuals have sought to capitalize on the popular demand for marked cross country routes by organizing trail associations, collecting large sums of money from our citizens in return for routing trails through their cities, and giving little service in return.*
>
> *We have also been informed that of the amounts collected in the various localities, one-third was allotted those communities to pay for marking the roads. The balance, or two-thirds of the funds collected was to be forwarded to the headquarters of the trail officials with the promise that the funds would be expended in advertising the cities through which these so-called trails pass.*
>
> *Devious, winding, and twisting routes have been selected through some communities to satisfy the wishes of the more enthusiastic contributors of funds, and the traveling public oftentimes has been seriously inconvenienced and misled.*

Realizing the importance of systematic, thorough, and judicious highway marking, this department has made a careful study of this subject, with the result that Illinois today has one of the most complete and comprehensive marking systems in the United States. Need for the specially marked trail in Illinois has passed; yet we are constantly besieged by the promoters of these organizations, and even by our own good citizens, who have been misled by the rosy picture of large financial returns by these promoters and organizers, to permit marking of new routes on the same highways which have already been paved and thoroughly marked by the state.

The matter is of such importance that it has been considered by the state board of highway advisers of Illinois, and by unanimous vote they have refused to approve any further trail markings.[109]

While not forbidding the continued operation of existing trail associations, the state was on record that there would be no more considered.

Later in 1925, Illinois and many other states across the country, working through the American Association of State Highway and Transportation Officials (AASHO), asked the U.S. secretary of agriculture to replace all trail names with a unified highway numbering system. Agriculture Secretary Howard M. Gore appointed the Joint Board on Interstate Highways, as recommended by AASHO, on March 2, 1925. The board was composed of twenty-one state highway officials and three federal Bureau of Public Roads officials. Their job was to plan a system of marked and numbered "interstate highways" across the country and develop a standardized design for a sign to mark these routes.

The board worked diligently at the task and held a number of meetings across the country with state officials and interested parties. A final report was presented on October 30, 1925, which called for the establishment of a system of 96,626 miles of designated highways across the country. North–south routes would receive an odd number, with the lowest numbers in the east and the highest in the west, and east–west routes an even number, with the lowest numbers in the south and the highest in the north. These routes were to be marked by a shield design with a white background and black numbers and lettering. On November 11, 1926, AASHO formally adopted the U.S. numbered highway system for implementation across the country. This set in motion the remarking of the designated highways and almost immediately rendered the named trails and their booster associations obsolete.[110]

As would be expected, the trail associations were not happy with this outcome, but the decision of the Lincoln Highway Association, the most

Intersection of US Route 45 and Illinois Route 9 in Champaign. Note the US Route 45 shield in foreground. *Champaign County History Museum.*

influential of the trail associations, to mark the end of its formal operations at the close of 1927 proved to be a symbolic end to the era. The Dixie Highway Association also disbanded in 1927, and it is not known exactly when the Egyptian Trail Association ceased operating, but it is believed it was about this same time. By this time, President Lumpkin would have been eighty-four years old, and Secretary-Treasurer Tucker had died suddenly earlier in 1927, so Lumpkin may not have been too upset about this, considering that the goals of his labors with the trail had come to fruition.

With the advent of the federal highway numbering system, the importance of the Egyptian Trail in this scheme was readily apparent. The Egyptian Trail, which had been included in portions of Illinois State Bond Improved Routes 2, 12 and 25, would now be identified as US Route 45 from Kankakee to Effingham, US Route 50 from Salem to Sandoval and US Route 51 from Sandoval to Cairo. This left two portions of the trail not under a federal number: the road from Watson to Salem, which ended up being identified as Illinois Route 37, and a yet-to-be improved route from Kankakee to Chicago.

Under the State Bond Improved routing, the Kankakee to Chicago portion of the trail was served by traffic heading east out of Kankakee to Momence and then utilizing the Dixie Highway or State Bond Improved Route 1 north to Chicago. This "detour" added extra mileage and cost time. By the end of the 1920s, motorists were looking for a more direct link

US Route logos. *Author's collection.*

to Chicago from Kankakee, and they found a supporter in Governor Len Small, a Kankakee native.

Small proposed a forty-foot concrete "superhighway" to be known as Illinois Route 49—alternately, as the Governors Highway—under his $100 million road bond issue approved by voters on November 4, 1924.[111] The road was to parallel the Illinois Central Railroad and travel north of Kankakee through Bradley, Matteson, Homewood and other towns, then north into Chicago along South Park Avenue and Halsted Street. Some initial work started on the highway in the fall of 1927.

To further work, a settlement was made by Kankakee and Will Counties with the bankrupt Chicago and Interurban Traction Company for the purchase of the old interurban right of way through the two counties on April 24, 1928. This allowed for the construction of the new highway along the old interurban line beginning at Indian Oaks, an unincorporated community just north of Kankakee, to Monee. As the interurban right of way was only fifty feet wide and a ninety-foot strip was needed for the highway, additional land needed to be acquired along this stretch. Landowners received a settlement of $250 per acre for these purchases. For most of this section, the highway was surveyed to run on the east side of the Illinois Central Railroad tracks. Just south of Monee, the highway made a large, sweeping curve and began to run on the west side of the railroad the remainder of the way to Chicago.[112]

In Cook County, purchases of the last six parcels for highway easements were not finalized until June 1929, and this helped move along final construction, particularly along a portion of the highway near Richton Park, which terminated in a cornfield and required a confusing detour.[113] By 1931, the final segments of paving were completed on Illinois Route 49—the Governors Highway—near Calumet Park and south of Monee near the Racoon Grove preserve.

In September 1932, it was announced that Illinois Route 49 north of Kankakee, and then Illinois Route 50 (Cicero Avenue) north of Monee, would be one of fourteen World's Fair Highways that would extend like "spokes of a wheel" about one hundred miles in every direction from Chicago. These highways would be marked with special signs designating them as a route to the 1933 Century of Progress—Chicago International Exposition, which was to take place from May 27, 1933, to November 12, 1933, and was later extended from May 26, 1934, to October 31, 1934. It was estimated that hundreds of thousands of pleasure-seekers would use these highways and that most undoubtedly would stop long enough along the way to buy gasoline, oil, other supplies and services for their cars, food, refreshments, tourist supplies and clothing, boosting the economies of the towns the highways passed through. Specially designed tourist camps also circled Chicago on a ten-mile radius, providing comfortable accommodations for auto travelers choosing not to patronize hotels in the city.[114]

Illinois Route 49 was named the "Midway Route" and was marked by signs featuring a clown.[115] Other World's Fair highways included: Roosevelt Road, the Illumination Route; Ogden Avenue, the Aero Route; State Highway 7 through Joliet, the Communication Route; State Highway 4 through Joliet, the Agriculture Route; U.S. Route 41 through Indiana, the Industrial Route; U.S. Route 6 through Indiana, the International Route; U.S. Routes 12/20 through Indiana, the Automotive Route; State Highway 19—Northwest Highway, the Railroad Route; State Highway 21 through Libertyville, the Radio Route; State Highway 68, the Electrical Route; State Highway 42 through Evanston, the Marine Route; and U.S. Route 20 through Elgin, the Fort Dearborn Route. Each of the routes had its own special symbol, and over fifteen thousand signs were used to mark the 1,500 miles of World's Fair highways.[116]

The World's Fair also served as a catalyst for the rebirth of the Egyptian name—this time, as the Egyptian Highway. In a meeting in Mattoon on March 13, 1933, a proposal was made to form the Egyptian Highway Association, described as a "perpetuation of the Old Egyptian Trail, which was formed, at the suggestion of Mattoon men, 18 years ago." The Egyptian Highway was to follow the old route from Chicago to Cairo, with one exception: south of Effingham, it would travel through Mt. Vernon, Marion and Mound City south to Cairo.

Two Mattoon men, H.R. Checkley and D.J. Twomey, served as president and secretary of the new association, respectively. Billing the Egyptian Highway as the "Shortest, Safest, Fastest Route—Cairo and Southern

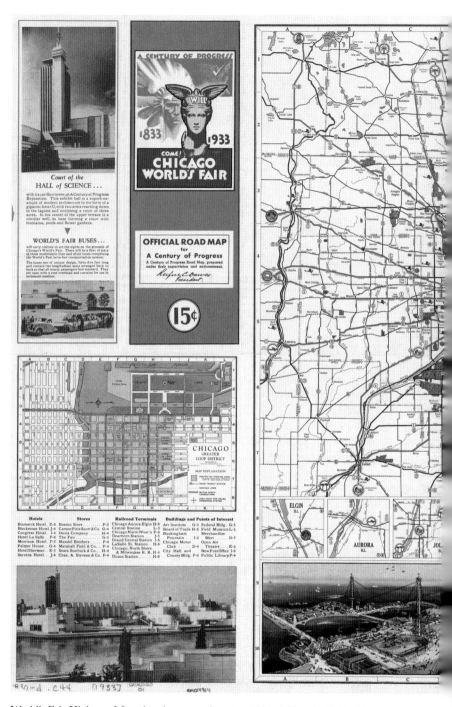

World's Fair Highway Map showing named routes, 1933. *Milwaukee Public Library.*

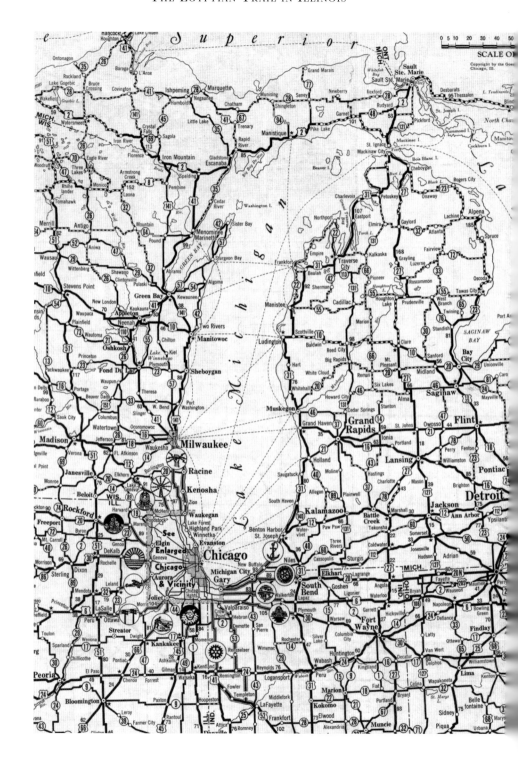

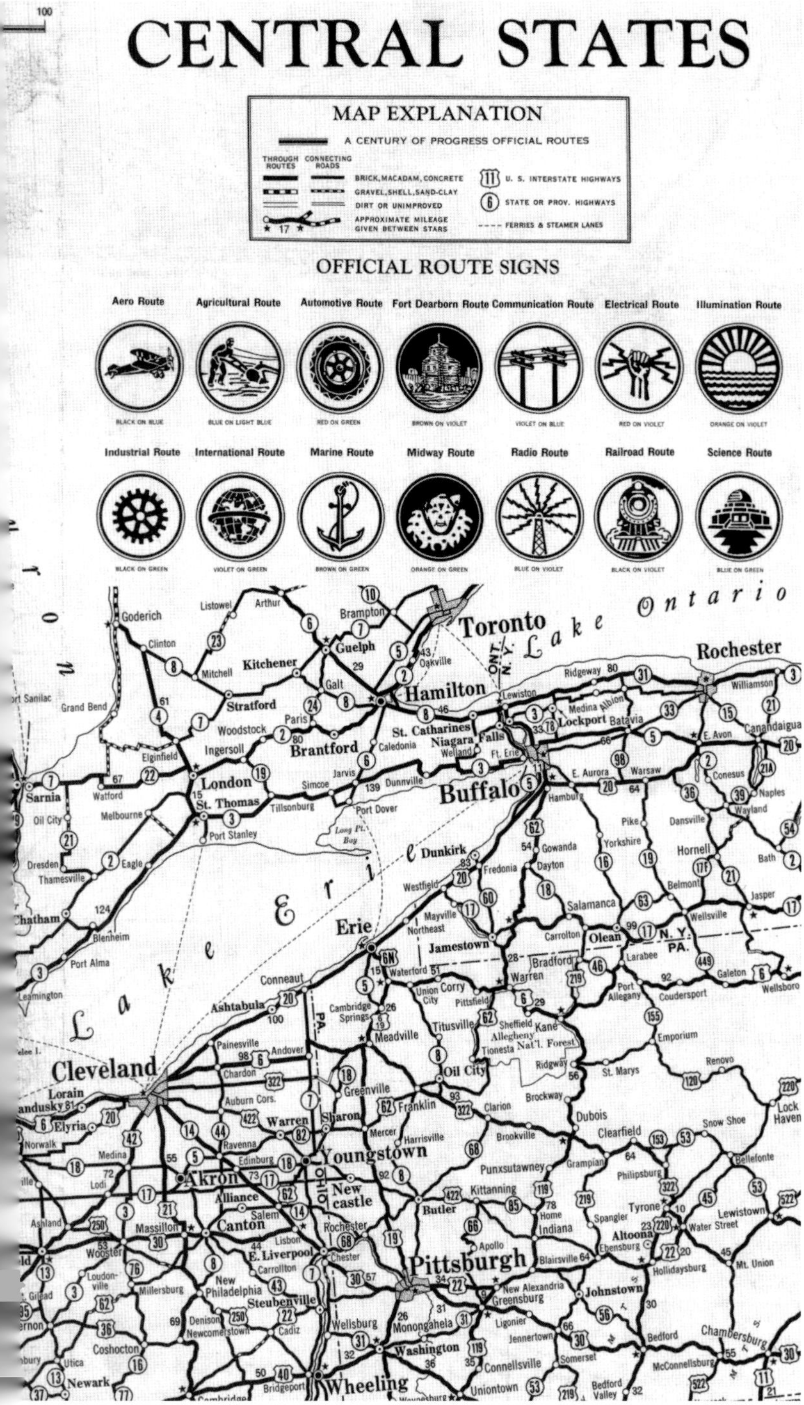

CENTRAL STATES

MAP EXPLANATION

A CENTURY OF PROGRESS OFFICIAL ROUTES

THROUGH ROUTES	CONNECTING ROADS	
		BRICK, MACADAM, CONCRETE
		GRAVEL, SHELL, SAND-CLAY
		DIRT OR UNIMPROVED

★ 17 ★ APPROXIMATE MILEAGE GIVEN BETWEEN STARS

11 U. S. INTERSTATE HIGHWAYS
6 STATE OR PROV. HIGHWAYS
----- FERRIES & STEAMER LANES

OFFICIAL ROUTE SIGNS

Aero Route — BLACK ON BLUE
Agricultural Route — BLUE ON LIGHT BLUE
Automotive Route — RED ON GREEN
Fort Dearborn Route — BROWN ON VIOLET
Communication Route — VIOLET ON BLUE
Electrical Route — RED ON VIOLET
Illumination Route — ORANGE ON VIOLET

Industrial Route — BLACK ON GREEN
International Route — VIOLET ON GREEN
Marine Route — BROWN ON GREEN
Midway Route — ORANGE ON GREEN
Radio Route — BLUE ON VIOLET
Railroad Route — BLACK ON VIOLET
Science Route — BLUE ON GREEN

Close-up view of signage for 1933 world's fair. *Milwaukee Public Library.*

Illinois to Chicago," the association published thousands of pocket-sized strip maps showing its route and included maps of the "Century of Progress" World's Fair and the Chicago Metropolitan area that were distributed throughout the state and region. The maps also included information on points of interest tourists could visit along the way.[117]

Plans were made to mark the highway route with circular signs displaying a stylized version of a pyramid, as well. These plans never received much traction, likely due to the edict the state had issued years earlier regarding not approving any new marked trails and also the fact that following the end of the fair in 1934, public interest in the Egyptian Highway waned, just as it did for the Egyptian Trail, and both names faded into obscurity.

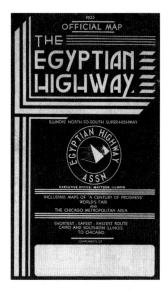

Egyptian Highway Association promotional flyer. *Author's collection.*

Although the Egyptian Highway may have faded into obscurity, Illinois Route 49—the Governors Highway—lived up to expectations that it would be a major trafficked through route to Chicago. Highway officials recognized this and redesignated the highway from Kankakee to Chicago as part of US Route 54 in 1941. US Route 54, at the time, ran in a southwesterly direction from Chicago, terminating near the Mexico border at El Paso, Texas, and traveled through the states of Illinois, Missouri, Kansas, Oklahoma, New Mexico and Texas. In Illinois, US Route 54

Interstate 57 logo. *Author's collection.*

entered the state near the town of Pittsfield on the Missouri border and passed though Springfield, Clinton, Onarga, Kankakee and others on the way to Chicago. Illinois 49—the Governors Highway—was designated as a federal highway until 1971 after the completion of Interstate 57. Following that, Illinois Route 49 was redesignated as part of Illinois Route 50 to just north of Monee, where Illinois Route 50 (Cicero Avenue) runs due north into Cook County. The remainder of Illinois Route 49 through Matteson, Flossmoor and Homewood was simply designated the Governors Highway

View of US Route 54 near Illinois/Missouri state line. *IDOT.*

and received no special highway number. These designations remain in place to this day.[118]

Interstate 57, part of the Eisenhower Interstate System, is the longest interstate highway in Illinois. It runs for approximately 359 miles in the state and parallels much of the original Egyptian Trail and Illinois Central Railroad routes between Cairo and Chicago, except that south of Salem, it travels through Mt. Vernon, Benton, Marion and Mound City south to Cairo.

The Interstate Highway System was part of the Federal-Aid Highway Act, signed by President Dwight D. Eisenhower on June 29, 1956, which authorized the construction of over forty thousand miles of limited-access highways nationwide. The Interstate Highway System gained its champion in President Eisenhower, who was influenced by his experiences as a young Army officer crossing the country in the 1919 Motor Transport Corps convoy that drove, in part, on the Lincoln Highway. He recalled, "The old convoy had started me thinking about good two-lane highways…the wisdom of broader ribbons across our land." Eisenhower also gained an appreciation of the Reichsautobahn system, Germany's modern highway network, as a necessary component of a national defense system while he was serving as supreme commander of the Allied Forces in Europe during World War II.

By 1959, the first portions of interstate highways had opened in Illinois, primarily on tollways such as Interstate 90 near Schaumburg to South Beloit and Interstates 94 and 294 in the Chicago area.[119]

The first construction contracts on Interstate 57 were awarded in 1957, with the initial 6.2-mile stretch of the highway completed between Bradley and Kankakee in early 1959. Two years later, a 33-mile stretch was finished between Wetaug and Marion and dedicated by Governor Otto Kerner in ceremonies on September 26, 1961. Construction of this completed section cost $37,500,000 or an average of $1,300,000 a mile.[120]

Gradually, over the next ten years, construction on Interstate 57 was completed on all sections of the highway. The final twenty-two-mile portion of the highway between Rantoul and Buckley was opened for traffic and dedicated in ceremonies in Paxton by Governor Richard Ogilvie on November 20, 1971.[121] Despite cold temperatures and cloudy skies, over three hundred people turned out for the ribbon-cutting ceremonies, where the Chanute Air Force Band played music for the "gala celebration." ("Great day to open a highway; two more coming Wednesday.")[122]

As the Egyptian Trail served as the basic template for the route of Interstate 57, there is no doubt this is certainly part of the legacy of the trail and a credit to the vision of President Lumpkin, Secretary-Treasurer Tucker and trail leaders. In a little over fifty years, the Egyptian Trail had gone, conceptually, from improved dirt roads to paved, two-lane state bond and US highways to a concrete, four-lane limited access highway.

Today, though there are few original road alignments in the state that still bear the Egyptian Trail name—chiefly near Monee and Peotone in Will County and Tuscola and Arcola in Douglas County—the impact and foresight of trail organizers has been longstanding. An effort made in the late 1990s led to the designation of sections of old US Route 51 in southern Illinois as the Historic Egyptian Trail. The initiative was spearheaded by Homer Forby, an Illinois Department of Transportation mechanic and mayor of Cobden at the time. Forby

Historic Egyptian Trail sign installed in later years along old US Route 51. *IDOT.*

Construction of Interstate 57 near Wetaug. *Illinois Secretary of State.*

Construction of Interstate 57 near Chebanse. *Illinois Secretary of State.*

Construction of Interstate 57 near Chebanse. *Illinois Secretary of State.*

enlisted the aid of Illinois State Representative Mike Bost, who drafted a resolution calling for portions of old US Route 51 from Carbondale to Cairo that were being realigned in a major road improvement project to be given the historic designation. The resolution passed unanimously in the Illinois House of Representatives on November 14, 1997.[123] Historic Road signs were made by the state department of transportation and installed along the designated route. Though few of these signs remain in place after a quarter century, the historic road signs are still included in the Illinois Standard Highway Signs Book (Illinois Standard XM-7) and can be easily reproduced and replaced along the historic route.

In fact, with a greater appreciation of the history of the Egyptian Trail, other portions of the Egyptian Trail, like the US Route 45 and US Route 50 sections of the highway, can also be considered for historic designation to help perpetuate the legacy of this long-forgotten roadway—perhaps one of the most important in the annals of Illinois transportation history.

HOUSE RESOLUTION 257 (adopted November 14, 1997)

WHEREAS, U.S. Route 51 was established in 1923 and was constructed over the preexisting portion of the roadway called Egyptian Trail in southern Illinois; and

WHEREAS, a new U.S. Route 51, from Carbondale to Cario, is being completed, which will abandon portions of old U.S. Route 51; therefore, be it

RESOLVED, BY THE HOUSE OF REPRESENTATIVES OF THE NINETIETH GENERAL ASSEMBLY OF THE STATE OF ILLINOIS, that those portions of old U.S. Route 51 in southern Illinois that have been abandoned by new U.S. Route 51 be named Egyptian Trail; and be it further

RESOLVED, That we respectfully request the Illinois Department of Transportation to erect, at suitable locations consistent with State and federal regulations, appropriate signs, markers, or plaques giving notice of the name; and be it further

RESOLVED, That a suitable copy of this resolution be presented to the Secretary of Transportation for the State of Illinois.

CAIRO

Though there is no dispute that Chicago is still that great "metropolis of the state in the north," the passage of well over a century has taken its toll on the city of Cairo.

Cairo was established in 1836 in the heart of "Little Egypt." At the confluence of the Mississippi and Ohio Rivers, Cairo lies in an area with the lowest elevation of any location within the state of Illinois. In 1855, Cairo became the terminus of the Illinois Central Railroad, and the town flourished as trade with Chicago spurred development. By 1860, the population exceeded two thousand.

During the Civil War, Cairo became a strategically important supply base and training center for the Union army, though much of the city's trade was diverted to Chicago. General Ulysses S. Grant even made his headquarters in Cairo from 1861 to 1862.

Due to Cairo's location, the town flourished after the war. It became a center for banking and an important steamboat port, with so much river traffic that the city was designated as a port of delivery by act of Congress in 1854. Moreover, Cairo became a hub for railroad shipping in the region. It was estimated that nearly five hundred thousand railroad cars were ferried across the rivers there in the late 1800s. Wealthy merchants and shippers were attracted to Cairo and built numerous fine mansions in the nineteenth and early twentieth centuries.

Bridge over the Ohio River south of Cairo. *IDOT.*

Cairo's population peaked in the 1920s, surpassing fifteen thousand people. By that time, however, ferry traffic had already started declining as the railroad was now able to cross the river after new bridges were constructed, and Cairo began to lose its importance as a transportation hub.

With river traffic and rail traffic drastically reduced, much of Cairo's shipping, railroad and ferry industries left the city, and employment prospects left with them. Racial tensions were strained by the late 1960s, as the nation was in the middle of the civil rights struggle. Racial violence, protests and riots between police and Cairo's Black community intensified the city's decline. In 1978, with the opening of a new bridge on Interstate 57 across the Mississippi River, Cairo was bypassed, and the town suffered further. Restaurants, hotels and even Cairo's hospital closed. Flooding further contributed to the town's demise.

By 2020, Cairo's population had fallen to only 1,733 people. Poverty, crime and unemployment remain challenges for the town, but in recent years, there have been attempts to restore some of Cairo's abandoned buildings to develop heritage tourism focusing on its history and its relationship to the Mississippi and Ohio Rivers. In 2021, the Cairo Historical Preservation Project was started to help preserve some of Cairo's most historic buildings, which include the Custom House Museum, Cairo Public Library, Magnolia Manor and the Ward Chapel AME Church.

NOTES

Chapter 1

1. Brockton G. Lange, *History of the Illinois Department of Transportation 1903–2013* (Springfield: Illinois Department of Transportation, 2013).
2. *Illinois Highway Improvement Bluebook* (Chicago: Illinois Highway Improvement Association, 1919).
3. Richard F. Weingroff, "A Peaceful Campaign of Progress and Reform: The Federal Highway Administration at 100," *Public Roads* 57, no. 2 (Autumn 1993).
4. Albert Brigham, "Good Roads in the United States," *Bulletin of the American Geographical Society* 36, no. 12 (1904): 728.
5. *America's Highways, 1776–1976* (Washington, D.C.: Federal Highway Administration, 1976), 48.
6. Ibid., 48–49.
7. *Report of the Office of Public Road Inquiries for 1901* (Washington, D.C.: United States Department of Agriculture, January 1902), 243.
8. Lange, *Illinois Department of Transportation*, 4.
9. Ibid., 6.
10. *Illinois Highway Improvement Bluebook*, 31.
11. Lange, *Illinois Department of Transportation*, 5.
12. *Annual Report of the Illinois Highway Commission for the Year 1907* (Springfield: Illinois State Highway Commission, 1907–08).

13. *Brief History of Township Government* (Springfield: Township Officials of Illinois, 2022).
14. Lange, *Illinois Department of Transportation*, 7.
15. *Illinois Official 1925 Auto Trails Map* (Springfield: Illinois Secretary of State—Automobile Department—Louis L. Emmerson, 1925).
16. *Illinois Highway Improvement Bluebook*, 13–15.
17. Lange, *Illinois Department of Transportation*, 12.
18. *Illinois Highway Improvement Bluebook*, 45.
19. "Marked Through Routes in Illinois," *Illinois Highways* 3 (July 1916), 74.
20. Larry A. McClellan, *The Pontiac Trail: Route 66 and the Chicago to St. Louis Roads* (Pontiac, IL: Pontiac Vintage Press, 2013), 33.
21. Richard F. Weingroff, "The Lincoln Highway," U.S. Department of Transportation Federal Highway Administration, https://www.fhwa.dot.gov/infrastructure/lincoln.cfm.

Chapter 2

22. "'Egyptian Trail' Conceived a Century Ago in Mattoon," *Effingham Daily News*, November 29, 2015.
23. "Consolidated Communications CELEBRATES 125 YEARS!," Consolidated Communications, https://www.consolidated.com/celebrating125.
24. "Auto Firm Moves into New Home, Mattoon Motor Car Company Invites Public Inspection," *Mattoon Journal-Gazette*, December 3, 1948.
25. "Damage of $8000 Done in Garage, Several Automobiles Badly Scorched by Flames in Mattoon Motor Car Company's Building," *Mattoon Journal-Gazette*, January 2, 1913.
26. "W.C. Lumpkin Meets Death, One of Mattoon's Most Prominent Citizens Killed in an Auto Accident," *Mattoon Journal-Gazette*, January 12, 1924; "Well Known Telephone Man Killed in Accident," *Bell Telephone News*, February 1924.
27. "Retired Physician and Businessman of Mattoon Dies, Dr. I.A. Lumpkin Succumbs Tuesday Afternoon," *Decatur Herald*, July 23, 1930.
28. "History of the Gazette—Mattoon's First Paper," *Mattoon Journal-Gazette*, February 12, 1909.
29. "Death Comes to E.B. Tucker at 9 a.m. Today, Officer of Journal Company Succumbs Following Operation," *Mattoon Journal-Gazette*, February 28, 1927.

30. "Our First Tour in an Automobile," *Rambler Magazine*, September 1905.
31. "Death Comes to E.B. Tucker."
32. "New Trail Is Mapped Out, Egyptian Trail Boosters from Illinois Central Cities Meet Here and Organize," *Mattoon Journal-Gazette*, June 15, 1915.
33. "Centralia Is a Division Point—Egyptian Trail, Will Have Meeting in Carbondale Soon to Organize," *Centralia Evening Sentinel*, June 17, 1915.
34. "Chicagoans in Favor—Through Auto Route Egyptian Trail Organization to Be Perfected at Meeting, Which Promises to be Enthusiastic One," *Mattoon Journal-Gazette*, June 14, 1915.
35. Lange, *Illinois Department of Transportation*.
36. "Egyptian Trail," *Paxton Record*, August 26, 1915.
37. "Danger Signs and Limit Posts for Egyptian Trail," *Centralia Evening Sentinel*, September 15, 1915.
38. Muriel Mueller Milne, *Our Roots Are Deep: A History of Monee, Illinois* (South Holland, IL, South Suburban Genealogical and Historical Society, 1973), 91.

Chapter 3

39. "Egyptian Trail Meeting This Afternoon at Courthouse; Officers," *Kankakee Daily Republican*, July 9, 1915.
40. "Halsted Street, Boosted for State Aid at a Rousing Meeting," *Riverdale Pointer*, October 15, 1915.
41. "Halsted Street May Be Made 'Egyptian Trail' and Dixie Route," *The Riverdale Pointer*, July 30, 1915.
42. "The Backbone for a Great System of Illinois Improved Highways—The Egyptian Trail," *Harvey Tribune*, October 15, 1915.
43. "Egyptian Trail Via Halsted Street, Harvey Delegation Gets What They Went After at Kankakee," *Harvey Tribune*, September 24, 1915; "Egyptian Trail—Halsted Street Selected as Route to City," *Riverdale Pointer*, September 24, 1915.
44. "Mass Meeting to Consider Hard Roads," *Peotone Vedette*, September 30, 1915.
45. "Personal and Local Items," *Paxton Record*, September 16, 1915.
46. "Egyptian Trail Boosters Meet in Kankakee," *Gilman Star*, September 23, 1915.
47. "Painters Notice," *Riverdale Pointer*, November 12, 1915.
48. "Homewood News," *Riverdale Pointer*, December 31, 1915.

49. "Egyptian Trail Markers Being Placed on Poles," *Peotone Vedette*, November 11, 1915.

50. *Official Automobile Blue Book—Volume Five—Illinois, Wisconsin, Minnesota, Iowa, and Missouri* (Chicago: Automobile Blue Book Publishing Company, 1917).

51. Unless otherwise noted, information for town descriptions throughout this book was taken from these sources: Edward Callary, *Place Names of Illinois* (Champaign: University of Illinois Press, 2008); *Illinois Counties & Incorporated Municipalities* (Springfield: Illinois Secretary of State, Department of Index, 1999); "Romance Found in Many Station Names, Illinois Pioneers Are Commemorated, as Are the Indians and the Company's Early Officials," *Illinois Central Magazine*, January 1922 (40–42); Wikipedia; and 1920 census data. Route descriptions are from 1915, when known.

52. *Peotone on Parade: 1856–1956*, published for Peotone's centennial celebration in 1956 by the Peotone Centennial General Committee and Historical Program Committee, available online, from the University of Illinois Urbana-Champaign library, https://libsysdigi. library.uiuc.edu/oca/Books2008-06/peotoneonparade100peot/ peotoneonparade100peot.pdf.

53. *The Tourists' Auto Guide of Illinois, Wisconsin, Michigan, Indiana* (Chicago: Inter-State Auto Guide Company, 1919).

54. Information from the City of Chicago, the Commission on Chicago Landmarks.

Chapter 4

55. New Trail Is Mapped Out, Egyptian Trail Boosters from Illinois Central Cities Meet Here and Organize," *Mattoon Journal Gazette*, June 15, 1915.

56. "New Trail Is Mapped Out, Boosters from Illinois Meet and Organize," *Paxton Record*, June 17, 1915.

57. Ibid.

58. "Sandoval Wants on Egyptian Trail," *Centralia Evening Sentinel*, July 7, 1915; "Sandoval Given Egyptian Trail Berth Yesterday," *Centralia Evening Sentinel*, July 8, 1915; "Egyptian Trail Heads Hold Meeting Here, Detailed Route from Paxton to Centralia Is Adopted at Gathering in Elks Club Room," *Mattoon Journal Gazette*, July 7, 1915.

59. "550 Boosters Attend Meeting, Great Enthusiasm Shown by Promoters of Southern Division of Egyptian Trail," *Carbondale Daily Free Press*, June 25, 1915.

60. "Farina News," *Centralia Evening Sentinel*, August 19, 1915.

61. "Business and Otherwise—Pope Motorcycles," *Champaign Daily News*, November 4, 1915.

62. "Alligators—Lots of 'Em," *Paxton Record*, April 23, 1915.

63. "Egyptian Trail," *Paxton Record*, August 26, 1915.

64. George Rippey Stewart, *Names on the Land: A Historical Account of Place-Naming in the United States* (Boston: Houghton Mifflin, 1967), 362.

65. Linda Brewer, *Tuscola: Strolling through the Past, 1857–2007: A Pictorial History* (Tuscola, IL: History Book Committee, 2007).

66. *Champaign Daily Gazette*, August 10, 1915.

67. *Scarborough's Official Tour Book—Indiana, Ohio, Michigan, Illinois, Wisconsin* (Indianapolis, IN: Scarborough Motor Guide Company, 1917), 283.

68. Ibid.

69. The Editors of Encyclopaedia Britannica, "Salem," Encyclopedia Britannica, November 29, 2016, https://www.britannica.com/place/Salem-Illinois.

70. J.H.G. Brinkerhoff, *Brinkerhoff's History of Marion County, Illinois* (Indianapolis, IN: Bowen, 1909), 187.

Chapter 5

71. "550 Boosters Attend Meeting."

72. "Carbondale Meet Was Great Boost for Good Roads," *Centralia Evening Sentinel*, June 25, 1915.

73. "Centralia Is a Division Point."

74. "Logan-Lee Highway," *Wyoming Post Herald*, September 13, 1916.

75. "Vice-Presidents Meet and Change Route to Ashley, Egyptian Trail between Richview and Ashley to Be Re-Logged, Will Not Detour Road to Radom and DuBois," *Centralia Evening Sentinel*, July 3, 1915.

76. "Buncombe," *Carbondale Daily Free Press*, September 15, 1915.

77. "Completing Plans for Egyptian Trail, Officers Settle on Route from Carbondale to Union County Line," *Carbondale Daily Free Press*, July 7, 1915.

78. "The Egyptian Trail," *Carbondale Daily Free Press*, August 3, 1915.

79. "Want Assistance in Making Road," *Carbondale Daily Free Press*, August 21, 1916.

80. "The Egyptian Trail," *Carbondale Free Press*, July 10, 1915.
81. "Boskydell's Sandstone Preserved in Region's Landmarks," *Southern Illinoisan*, July 9, 2010.
82. *Official Automobile Blue Book*, 307.
83. *Scarborough's Official Tour Book*, 278.
84. Information from the Archives Center, National Museum of American History.

Chapter 6

85. "To Improve Egyptian Trail," *Paxton Record*, August 23, 1917.
86. *Illinois Highway Improvement Bluebook*, 47–49.
87. Ibid., 55.
88. "House Passes Bill," *Mt. Carmel Daily Republican Register*, April 12, 1917.
89. *Illinois Highway Improvement Bluebook*, 103–7.
90. Lange, *Illinois Department of Transportation*, 16.
91. *Illinois Highway Improvement Bluebook*, 58–59.
92. Ibid., 59.
93. "Illinois Hard Road Bonds Sold Strong," *Macomb Daily By-Stander*, October 25, 1921.
94. "Road in 1921, State May Not Touch Egyptian Trail Until Spring 1921," *Paxton Record*, January 29, 1920.
95. Lange, *Illinois Department of Transportation*, 16.
96. "Put Hard Roads Up to People," *Paxton Record*, November 30, 1917.
97. "Egyptian Trail Is Likely to Be Followed," *Mattoon Journal Gazette*, April 17, 1920.
98. "Attention Egyptian Trail Boosters," *Carbondale Free Press*, September 14, 1920.
99. Untitled article, *Decatur Herald Review*, February 4, 1923.
100. "Buckley News," *Paxton Record*, March 29, 1923.
101. "Egyptian Trail Route," *Paxton Record*, May 3, 1923.
102. "Hard Work Progresses," *Paxton Record*, July 19, 1923.
103. "New Record Hung Up by McNeely Co.," *Mattoon Journal Gazette*, August 15, 1923.
104. "Construction Company Using Two Mixers," *Paxton Record*, October 18, 1923.
105. "Move Paxton Residence to Make Way for Hard Road," *Paxton Record*, November 1, 1923.

106. "Governor to Be Present at Road Opening," *Effingham Democrat,* October 11, 1923.

107. Lange, *Illinois Department of Transportation*, 18.

108. *Chicago Daily Tribune*, November 15, 1957.

Chapter 7

109. "State Officials Put End to New Trail Markings," *Chicago Daily Tribune,* February 8, 1925.

110. *Report of Joint Board on Interstate Highways October 30, 1925* (Washington, D.C.: United States Department of Agriculture, November 1925).

111. "$100,000,000 for More Highways in Illinois," *Highway Engineer and Contractor* 9 (October 1923).

112. Milne, *Our Roots Are Deep*, 99.

113. "All Right of Way for Highway 49 Negotiated," *Chicago Tribune,* June 23, 1929.

114. "Belvidere Is Out of Route to World Fair," *Belvedere Daily Republican,* September 12, 1932.

115. Milne, *Our Roots Are Deep*, 99.

116. "Belvidere Is Out of Route."

117. "New Highway Body Perpetuates Organization," *Mattoon Journal Gazette*, March 11, 1934.

118. Milne, *Our Roots Are Deep*, 99.

119. Illinois Secretary of State, "Interstate 57 Construction Photographs 1965–1966," https://www.ilsos.gov/departments/archives/online_exhibits/100_documents/1965-66-int57-photos.html.

120. "Dedication at Marion," *Southern Illinoisian*, September 25, 1961.

121. "Interstate 57 Section to Open November 20," *Decatur Herald and Review*, November 6, 1971.

122. "Great Day to Open a Highway; Two More Coming Wednesday," *Pantagraph*, November 21, 1971.

123. Family interviews with Anna Forby and Lynn Forby Gesky.

ABOUT THE AUTHOR

 James R. Wright was a local historian and author. He was a member of the Homewood Historical Society for forty years and a longtime scholar of the Prairie State's transportation heritage. His previous work includes *The Dixie Highway in Illinois*. Mr. Wright passed away in March 2023 before seeing the publication of *The Egyptian Trail in Illinois*.